"I frequently refer to my interactions with 'getting juiced up – refuelling my tank.' His ab the complex technical and business issues w yet keep us focused on what will truly sustain us in the future, is remarkable."

– **Len Fantasia, Vice President, Quality & Compliance Services Worldwide, Johnson & Johnson**

Praise for *Making Sense of Strategy*

"*Making Sense of Strategy* is a brief but highly useful discussion of modern strategic management from the perspective of an experienced practitioner. Tony Manning is able to take many commonly held ideas in strategy and weave them into a simple, yet elegant tapestry for appreciating the art of management ... The book is recommended for MBA programs, especially executive MBA programs, and all managers who doubt their impact on the long-term success of the firm. For anyone wishing to make an organization more effective, reading *Making Sense of Strategy* will be an hour well spent."

– **Jeffrey P. Katz,** *Academy of Management Executive*

"Good strategy is based on only a few principles and Manning has captured them all. The shortest strategy read available, yet still comprehensive. The perfect companion for the busy executive."

– **Professor Andrew Campbell, Director, Ashridge Strategic Management Centre, London**

Praise for *Discovering the Essence of Leadership*

"The book is an astonishing mixture of inspiration and practical business advice ... It is the finest work available for the busy businessperson who wants to get to grips with the subject."

– Wessel Ebersohn, *Succeed*

Praise for *Competing Through Value Management*

"An easily readable book, a useful tool for enabling managers to get a step ahead of the competition – a must read for managers at all levels." – Rob Sampson, *Saturday Dispatch*

Tony Manning's Management Toolkit

Tony Manning's Management Toolkit

Published by Zebra Press
an imprint of Struik Publishers
(a division of New Holland Publishing (South Africa) (Pty) Ltd)
PO Box 1144, Cape Town, 8000
New Holland Publishing is a member of Johnnic Communications Ltd

www.zebrapress.co.za

First published 2004

3 5 7 9 10 8 6 4

Publication © Zebra Press 2004
Text © Tony Manning 2004

Illustrations on pages 23 and 59 © Microsoft clipart

All rights reserved. No part of this publication may be reproduced,
stored in a retrieval system or transmitted, in any form or by any means,
electronic, mechanical, photocopying, recording or otherwise,
without the prior written permission of the copyright owners.

PUBLISHING MANAGER: Marlene Fryer
MANAGING EDITOR: Robert Plummer
COVER AND TEXT DESIGNER: Natascha Adendorff
TYPESETTER: Natascha Adendorff
PRODUCTION CONTROLLER: Valerie Kommer

Set in 9.5 pt on 15 pt Stone Serif

Reproduction by Hirt & Carter (Cape) (Pty) Ltd
Printed and bound by Paarl Print, Oosterland Street, Paarl, South Africa

ISBN 1 86872 912 5

For Sandy and Lee
Thanks for being there
And being you –
And bringing so much
To my life

Contents

Introduction   13

Thanks, David Ogilvy   17
The critical question   21
The "ten-buck test"   21
Critical mass   23
Your "*don't* do" list   24
Just say no   26
Strategy 101   26
Simplicity   28
Involvement   30
Choice, not chance   31
Take charge!   33
Great performance is not normal   34
Attitude   35
What you know   36
What if…?   37
Beginner's mind   38
Repeatability   40
Break that pattern!   41
Strategy, leadership, and change   42
Skills of the strategist   45
Strategic IQ   48
Communication   49
Strategic conversation   51
The ValuePlan   54
Plan to talk   56
Pick your "hill"   57

Your "right" customer	59
Value	61
Results that matter	62
Any number will do	63
Define your "difference"	64
Sources of advantage	65
20 questions	66
Positioning	68
Focus, value, costs	69
The "results machine"	70
Growth choices	71
Opportunity search	72
Let's talk about people	74
Strategic horizons	76
Creating tomorrow today	78
Embracing paradox	79
Frame your view	82
Thinking about the future	83
The "five whys"	88
Fit to fight	89
Strategy and spirit	91
Speed	92
Budgeting games	93
Structure	94
Design for performance	96
Leadership	100
Did you hire these idiots?	101

Conditions for greatness	103
Trust	104
Teamwork	105
Reputation	107
Integrity	109
Culture	111
Climate	114
Pivotal people	115
Diversity	116
Creative thinking	118
Everyone a genius	121
Reflection on learning	122
The limits of freedom	123
Start slow, finish fast	124
The best time for decisions	125
Follow through	126
Your point of view	128
Draw a line in the sand	129
The move after next	130
The strategy staircase	130
Appendix 1	**133**
Appendix 2	**136**

Introduction

I've been working as a consultant to big companies for almost 20 years. I've also written a lot about management. Along the way, I've sat in thousands of meetings, read hundreds of books and thousands of articles, attended business school programmes and conferences, and spent countless hours reflecting on what I've seen, heard, and read. And one question keeps buzzing in my head:

*If management is so hard,
why do we complicate it even more?*

The world is a complex place. Things are always changing, and a small shift here triggers tidal waves over there. Competition in every industry is increasingly hostile – and often comes from outside your industry. Speed is everything. If you don't move and improve faster than the other guy, you get mowed down.

At the same time, organizations are living things. People are their basic building block, and people behave in strange ways. One minute they get on with each other, the next minute they're at each other's throats. They can be charming, creative, cooperative, and candid – or a pain in the ass.

The task of management is somehow to make sense of what's happening outside, and then to get the right things happening inside. Neither is easy. And many of the "tools" touted as being just the thing for the job are not helpful. In fact, some are not only downright useless, they're also dangerous.

For many years, I've held the view that business performance is held back by the very people who purport to know how to improve it. Of course, executives must get the blame. But they're not always helped by the gurus who offer help. A typical business school education, for example, offers a mind-numbing array of tools. Books, magazines, and training programmes add confusion. Ask the average manager, "What three ideas work best for you?" and he'll be stuck for an answer. Ask three executives the same question, and you'll be thoroughly confused.

Good management is essential to companies and countries. Developing good managers has to be a priority. The process would be dramatically accelerated if less time were spent on learning about exotic tools and more on *using* the ones that actually make a difference. Most of the concepts we need have been around for decades. When we ignore them or use them badly, we run into trouble. Trying something newer and flashier doesn't help.

When managers talk strategy, they almost always have a "language" problem. There are two reasons for this:

1. They use the same terms to mean different things because they understand concepts differently. "Core competence" means one thing to Jim and another to Penny. "Low cost operator," "customer intimacy," and "value migration" are interpreted in various ways.
2. Their experience makes them champions or sceptics of various ideas. One fancies a theory just published in the *Harvard Business Review*. Another attended a business school course where she got hooked on a particular jargon. A third has just finished a bestselling business book – and he's sure it holds the real answers to life.

The result is that people spend a lot of time talking past each other. They also waste time wrestling over which *techniques* to use – "We need a new vision and mission" ... "Let's do a SWOT analysis" ... "What about some scenarios?" ... "Why don't we try brainstorming?" ... "Wouldn't all this work better if we broke into small groups?"

My purpose in this small book is to give you a toolkit worth carrying.

One that'll help you get past language barriers and concept wars, so you can focus on important issues and deal with them in the easiest and best way.

You can dip into it wherever you like. Maybe you have a problem to solve: you'll find answers here to many of the questions executives face every day. Maybe you want to get a specific message to your troops: there are plenty of those as well. Or maybe you want a quote, a questionnaire, a framework, or a concept for your next meeting. Look no further.

There's a lot of meat in these 140 pages. There's stuff on the new business arena, strategy, organizational design, people, and much else. But no fat.

No manager needs all these tools all the time. Questions that are critical for one company at a particular time may not be important at another time – or to another company. A model or framework that helps you may not be what someone else needs. At some stage, though, every executive needs to think about everything here.

Your experience in using these ideas is of immense value to me, so if you want to tell me about it, I'd appreciate hearing from you. My e-mail address is strategy@tonymanning.com.

TONY MANNING
APRIL 2004

Thanks, David Ogilvy

I never knew David Ogilvy, but he changed my life.

When I was 21, I got a job selling advertising space. I needed to know roughly what I was talking about, so I went hunting for a book that might tell me. Luckily, I soon found a copy of *Confessions of an Advertising Man*, Ogilvy's autobiography. Right away I knew I wanted to be a copywriter.

Ogilvy was famous for saying things like, "The consumer is not a moron, she's your wife." He got rich and famous by creating ads for Shell, Dove soap, and Hathaway shirts. He became my hero because he wrote crisply and with great style, but more so because he was so utterly sure of his point of view.

The ad industry is fuelled by mystique. Strange people who clearly don't know what they're talking about regularly persuade clients to spend huge sums on campaigns that may or may not work. Executives who'd normally call for detailed feasibility studies and cost-benefit analyses sign off lavish TV commercials and print ads as if they were committing to an ice cream. But Ogilvy – who once was a stove salesman and then a market researcher – brought rare certainty, structure, and clarity to his craft.

He stood out because he was so sure of how advertising worked. He set out principles where others spouted platitudes. He used lots of lists and rules. His advice ranged from short copy to long baths, and it all made such good sense.

At least, I thought it did. So I wrote to him, and asked what other books I should read to help me become a copywriter.

His list was short: *The Art of Plain Talk*, by Dr Rudolph Flesch; *Reality in Advertising*, by Rosser Reeves; *Scientific Advertising*, by Claude Hopkins; and *Advertising That Works*, by John Caples.

Flesch's book was a simple version of his PhD thesis. Through careful study, he'd developed a recipe for readable writing (now used in Microsoft Word). From him, I learned to use short words, short sentences, and short paragraphs; to start sentences with "and" and "but"; to avoid adjectives; and to write actively, with plenty of punctuation marks. He led me to read all of Hemingway and Steinbeck and to study the easy style in *Reader's Digest*, *The New Yorker*, and the *New York Times*.

Reeves, Hopkins, and Caples were all copywriters. Like Ogilvy, they all based their ideas on research. They tested everything. Hunches had no place in their worlds unless they got the nod from customers. "We know what is most effective," said Hopkins (in 1923), "and we act on basic laws."[1]

These men were my early mentors. Much later, I discovered Peter Drucker, and from the first book I was hooked. I found in his writing a magical lode of insights simply revealed. Example: "The test of a healthy business is not the beauty, clarity, or perfection of its organization structure. It is the performance of people."[2]

Drucker wrote that in 1973. Now, 30 years later, managers are waking up to the fact. Imagine the cost of what they missed or ignored!

Remarkable insights fill all Drucker's works. In fact, almost everything that any guru has written over the past 50 years was probably first said – and *better* said – by him. "He jokes that his ideas 'have only one moving part,'" says Jack Beatty in *The World According to Peter Drucker*.[3] This is why he's had such an impact for so long.

---

1 Claude Hopkins, *Scientific Advertising*, New York City: Lord & Thomas, 1923
2 Peter F. Drucker, *Management Tasks, Responsibilities, Practices*, London: William Heinemann Ltd, 1973
3 Jack Beatty, *The World According to Peter Drucker*, New York: The Free Press, 1998

The years I spent in advertising and marketing taught me the value of the KISS principle: "Keep It Simple Stupid!" I also discovered the power of mnemonics: those mental "hooks" that grab and hold people's attention and snag in their memories. And I learned to combine words and pictures to make messages that have impact. So in my writing and presentations I try to stick to these rules:
1. Start with a clear idea of what you want to say;
2. Use words to draw pictures – or use pictures instead of words;
3. Keep it simple;
4. Use real-life examples;
5. Be human;
6. Repeat yourself in different ways.

The years I've spent as a management consultant have taught me the value of reducing issues to their essence, of digging past the surface to get to the underlying truth, and of hacking away at buzzwords and bluster until you're left with that "one moving part." So here's a checklist that should be on every executive's wall:
1. Start with the question: "What's the question?"
2. Get the real facts – and get all of them;
3. Demand a second "right" answer;
4. Insist on a range of options;
5. Keep asking, "How do you know?" "Why is that so?" "Who said?" "Where's the proof?";
6. Use the Japanese technique of the "five whys" (ask, "Why?" until you're happy there's not another answer);*
7. Be alert for flaky thinking camouflaged by fine words or fancy presentations.

---

* More about this on page 88.

In 1986, I was lucky enough to be included in a week-long facilitation workshop run by Carl Rogers. At the time, he was probably the most famous psychologist in the world. His influence on me was profound. A wonderful, gentle man, he taught me that communication is about creating "shared meaning," so two or more people understand things in exactly the same way. This, he said, requires that you listen more than you talk. More specifically, it requires *empathic* listening – that you stay silent while others find their deepest thoughts, that you let them hear themselves speak, that you give them space to change their own minds. And that you listen not just to their words but also to their feelings.

Ogilvy, Flesch, Reeves, Hopkins, and Caples aren't names that appear in MBA reading lists. Drucker is sneered at by many academics, and young managers prefer Michael Porter, Gary Hamel, Jim Collins, and Adrian Slywotzky. Carl Rogers is not a name they know.

What a pity. For while many of today's management experts do have much to contribute, it's too easy to assume that what they tell us is brand new, and that tomorrow someone else will have an even better idea.

There are few new insights about management. The most profound thinkers are not all newcomers. The best ideas for managers often come from other fields.

The fact is, there are few new insights about management. The most profound thinkers are not all newcomers. The best ideas for managers often come from other fields. So before you reach for the next magic bullet, pause and consider seven great men who said it all so long ago. And consider others you know whose ideas might be just what you need.

20 THANKS, DAVID OGILVY

The critical question

A manager's day is full of dilemmas. Your ability to come up with decent answers is a key measure of your worth. But beware of offering the right answer to the wrong thing. Be precise about what you're faced with, and about what's expected of you. All answers are born from questions, and the most critical question in business is:

"What is the question?"

That's always the first question to ask, and often the hardest one to answer. Ask it when you think through issues on your own. Ask it in meetings, or when you get into an argument. Ask it in project reviews, in brainstorming sessions, and when you evaluate new product ideas, an IT proposal, or a new ad campaign. And don't let people skip it or skirt it. Insist on a simple, straight, and clear answer before you move ahead.

The "ten-buck test"

We all wake up in the morning to a simple challenge:

"Where shall I place my bet today?"

This question bedevils us as managers, and in our personal lives. Even those of us who think we're superhuman have limited physical and mental resources. We have 24 hours in a day. We have a finite amount of money. And there's a hell of a lot to do.

So where to apply ourselves?

Should we go to work ... read a book ... hit the beach ... meet friends for coffee? And if we do opt for work, should we attend yet another technical meeting ... explore a new market ... sign off a new project ... interview someone for an important job? Or what?

Because we have too few resources and too many opportunities, we have to make choices and trade-offs. To try to do everything is futile.

The Italian economist Vilfredo Pareto saw this a century ago and made the 80/20 principle famous. It applies to every area of our lives. We put 80 per cent of our resources into stuff that gives us 20 per cent of our results, and just 20 per cent into things that give us an 80 per cent return. Every business decision hinges on this principle and most decision-makers in business are well aware of it. Yet most of us persist in trying to defy it.

> Because we have too few resources and too many opportunities, we have to make choices and trade-offs. To try to do everything is futile.

Instead of trying to use few resources to get big results, we use lots of resources to achieve precious little. Examples:

- We throw time, energy, and money at projects that will have little or no payoff;
- We chase customers who won't spend much with us;
- We labour to improve things that will make hardly any difference;
- We persist in training and mentoring people who'll never be anything but mediocre;
- We invest in products that'll never win meaningful market share, and won't survive for long.

As a strategist, imagine that you have ten bucks in your hand right now. How will you spend it? Which customers, products, processes, and people will get it? Which partnerships will you work at? Which promotional activities will you support?

What are you going to do first today? What should your colleagues do? You need to come back to this question again and again. And you need

to be tough about where you lay your bets. It's easy to use your ten bucks on customers who don't give you a hard time (but also don't spend), on publicity that gives you a warm feeling (but sells nothing), or on team-building programmes that hype everyone up (but fail to get them working together). Spending on the right things is much harder.

First, you have to identify them. Then, you have to turn your back on everything else. And you have to be resolute, because you'll be pressured to change.

Critical mass

Two words should be prominent in every office and factory:

Critical mass.

If you want to achieve anything in your personal life – write a book, run the Comrades, get a degree, earn a promotion – you have to commit whatever it takes. That usually means time. It can also mean money and effort. And it always involves *sacrifice* (trying to write a book while you train for the Comrades is not a good idea).

If you invest too little, you'll never succeed. Meeting any goal requires a critical mass of resources. In other words, *enough* of them.

It's the same in business:

- To get a new business going, you have to put in *enough* thought, effort, and money;
- To be competitive, you have to build *enough* capability in a key area such as product development, marketing, or after-sales service;
- To grow, you need *enough* customers, spending enough with you;
- To own a market, you have to spend *enough* on innovation, promotion, distribution, service, and so on.

In all things, it's important to reach critical mass as fast as possible. This doesn't mean you should throw resources at every task. But it does underline the need to pick your opportunities carefully, to tackle a few things at a time, and then to go at them with a vengeance.

Critical mass lets you get traction. Traction lets you gain momentum. Then, you keep rolling.

Your "don't do" list

What are you *not* going to do today?

What are you going to *stop* doing?

Any time you decide what you *will* do, you decide by implication what you *won't* do. The trouble is, none of us readily lets go. We'd rather hang on to activities than ditch them. We stay with people, projects, processes, and products too long. We cling to useless assets. We remain in empty, dysfunctional, or toxic relationships.

Deciding what to do has little effect without serious *commitment*. You have to put money on the table. And you have to take a lot of things off your "to do" list.

This is a tough call for any organization:

- What if you give up on a customer who decides tomorrow to splash out and spend a fortune?
- What if you call a halt to a project that might transform your business?
- What if you stop pursuing a deal that's bogged down, but would be worth a fortune if you could pull it off?
- What if you kill a new product when another burst of advertising could make it a blockbuster?
- What if you get rid of someone after spending a fortune on developing them, when in another week – or another job – they might prove to be brilliant?

Deciding what to do has little effect without serious *commitment*.

These are difficult judgments executives have to make all the time. It's usually easier *not* to make them – or at least, to delay them. It's also very stupid.

The longer you wait, the harder it gets.* "Sunk costs" mount, day by day. Money is just one of them; emotion makes people even more obstinate.

---

* Later, we'll look at when it's best *not* to act.

Just say no

Given the pressure for new ideas in business, it's tempting to say yes to every one of them that hits your desk. But it's often smarter to say no.

Adding to your "to do" list is easy. Spreading your bets looks like a way to deal with risk. Fans of "real options" say you should create a range of strategies, so you can pick or choose as the future becomes clear.

However, what seems to be a valuable portfolio of projects quickly turns out to be like a school of piranhas in a feeding frenzy. Each of them only has to take a few small bites of your budget to rip it apart.

Nothing costs nothing. The five minutes you spend on one activity is stolen from somewhere else. Cash you spend here can't be invested over there. Put one product on a retailer's shelf, and you may battle to get space for another. Service customer A, and customer B has to wait.

It takes guts to reject new proposals or to dump those already under way – especially after *you've* been the one to call for action. But someone has to do it. Poor leaders let their organizations get so busy they can't make money. Good ones just say no.

Strategy 101

Before you start your next strategy meeting, pin these guidelines on the wall:

1. The purpose of strategy is to capture and keep customers who are right for your business, and to earn more than your cost of capital doing it.

2. Customers must see a difference in your product or service that makes your offering more attractive than competitors', and matters enough to them that they'll pay your price for it. So you have to be damned good at *something*, and be known for it.
3. Ideally, you should try to own the most profitable turf in your competitive arena. To do this, you have to (a) *decide* where you want to be, (b) *position* yourself apart from your competitors, and (c) *hold* that position in customers' minds over time. In practice, that might be impossible. Your only "sustainable advantage" might be your ability to *execute* your strategy better than anyone else.
4. In both designing and executing your strategy, you have to make trade-offs. (It's impossible to be all things to all people, to do everything for everyone, or to do everything well!)

Strategy hinges on three questions:
1. Who is our "right" customer?
2. What value will we offer?
3. How will we do it?

Get those right, and everything else falls into place. Get them wrong, and you'll waste time, effort, and money – and never be competitive.

Precision is important. The more specific you are with your answers, the better.

If you face limited competition, you may get away with some vagueness. But as you face more players, and as hostility grows, you need to become increasingly exact. Careful analysis can often expose opportunities, even in a crowded field.

Strategy is not rocket science. But designing and executing an effective strategy can be extremely hard

> **As you face more players, and as hostility grows, you need to become increasingly exact.**

STRATEGY 101   27

to do. Both require foresight, insight, creativity, courage, decisiveness, commitment, and perseverance.

These are all human qualities, so the better the team you apply to the job, the better for you. A "community of champions" has a much better chance of success than a bunch of also-rans. You owe it to your company to involve the best and the brightest in thinking about your strategy. And also to build as much depth into your team as possible, so they can execute with excellence.

Simplicity

Managing just about any business is a complicated business. You have to juggle a lot of issues, make decisions with too little information, get bolshy people to work together, satisfy snotty customers, meet impossible deadlines, deal with unreasonable stakeholders – and still make money.

Doing business is hard enough without making it harder than it need be. It doesn't take much to paralyse an organization. Confusion is a natural state of affairs, and it gets worse as companies grow.

Executives are often their own worst enemies. They complicate the easiest of matters. Instead of clarity, they create confusion. Instead of making issues easy to understand, they make things difficult. Instead of making their strategies clear, they make them fuzzy and impossible to execute.

It's easy to stop people from doing the very things you expect them to do. The line between encouragement and discouragement is a thin one; the difference between barriers and pathways is often hard to see.

You can turn great performers into bumbling nitwits much faster than you can turn fools into stars.

What you *do* as a manager might be complicated, but the *tools* for doing it are quite simple. Most of them have been around for a hell of a long time. They probably have new names, but the underlying principles haven't changed.

Putting things simply may seem neither sophisticated nor smart. But there's no point in forcing people to de-code what you're saying. You can't create shared meaning if no one understands you. Mission statements, management concepts, and action plans are worthless if no one gets their drift.

What you *do* as a manager might be complicated, but the *tools* for doing it are quite simple.

You owe it to your colleagues to make things understandable. You owe it to your other stakeholders, too – and it's the only way to win their votes.

Beware, though, of easy answers. They're seductive, but not always right. And while you strive to make things simple, remember to guard against being *simplistic* – so naive and crude about matters that you hide their complexity. This is stupid, not clever. It misleads people and deludes them into thinking that issues exist in neat isolation. Then, they fail to see linkages or to understand that every move they make has unintended repercussions.

Simplicity must emerge from a holistic perspective. You need to see the big picture before you narrow your options and focus on one key issue or another. And as your strategy unfolds, your view needs to shift constantly between context, options, choices, actions, and results.

Involvement

The purpose of every business is to deliver profits over time. The purpose of organization is to multiply the efforts of individuals. The purpose of strategy is to make a firm a better "results machine" than its competitors. The purpose of executives (leaders, managers, or whatever else you choose to call them*) is to get results through people.

Simple, isn't it? And did you notice that it all comes down to *people*? So ask yourself this:

Who do you involve in shaping your strategy, and when?

Common practice is for a few top people to do the important thinking, then to send instructions to the rest. If "the rest" run into trouble or see a need to do something different, they ask for permission. This division of labour is supposed to make the results machine hum. In fact, it's like sand in the gears.

Strategy focuses effort on opportunities. Action exposes opportunities and affects strategy. So strategy and action are inextricably linked. Companies are learning that even the best strategy is useless if it's not executed well. They're also learning that the boss and a few of his close colleagues can't make that happen. It takes a team.

The deeper that team's talents, the better. The more team members you involve in key decisions, the more likely you'll get the results you seek. And the more you involve them, the more you'll develop your pool of talent.

The message is clear:

---

* For more on this silly debate, see my book *Discovering the Essence of Leadership*, Zebra Press, 2002.

*Competitiveness is a people thing.
If you want to win,
you need to make your people winners.*

To tap their imagination and spirit, you have to give them information, respect, and resources. This is surely not hard to do. And now is surely the best time to do it.

Choice, not chance

The future will be what mankind makes it. As human beings, we have extraordinary power to shape it. Every one of us plays a part. Managers have a special responsibility to create the conditions that will benefit not only their organizations, but society as a whole. Strategically, it is in their interests to exert their influence.

Through good times and bad times, business results are largely a matter of choice, not chance. Everything will never go entirely your way. It's how you respond that counts.

Chance does play a role, of course, and can drive sales and profits up or down. Bad things happen to good companies. Good things happen when you least expect them.

Everything will never go entirely your way. It's how you respond that counts.

Many firms owe a large measure of their success to lucky breaks. Every executive should do all she can to prepare her firm to take advantage of luck – and should always be alert for signs of it.

But what really makes the difference over time is the *choices* managers make – or don't make – every day. Your decisions about products and services, markets, processes, investments, and so on are all commitments that define the future. Each of them paves the way to something else.

Choices like these have an immediate impact on your organization. But as a strategist, you also have to consider how they affect the world around you – and what their long-term implications might be. For actions you take to make your company better off today can have a profound influence on the larger business arena many years from now. They can determine whether you'll succeed or fail in a time you cannot yet see.

The way you treat your people will shape your company's reputation as an employer. The service you give customers will determine your future sales. The support you give your community will make you appreciated or reviled. Your contacts with government will cause you to be seen as a valuable partner, a nuisance, or a foe.

Since you can't see the future, you have to make judgments about what to do here and now and what it will mean in a week, a month, or ten years from now. This is an awesome responsibility. Seize it with both hands, and you may make the world a better place. Shirk it, and you'll have to take your chances. Along with the rest of us.

No one can change everything.
But every one of us can change
our bit of the world.

Take charge!

As a stream of choices flies at you, you can respond in one of two ways: *deliberately*, or by *default*.

The first mode is anticipatory and proactive. You work hard to understand what lies ahead and to create options for action – and you act in good time. The second mode is laid back and reactive. You let the future unfold as it will, deal with issues as they arise, and hope for the best.

Both paths are risky. You can be far-seeing, methodical, and bold, yet make the wrong move at the wrong time. Or you can bumble along and succeed spectacularly.

By the law of averages, however, you'll usually be best off if you take charge. When you duck the responsibility of choosing what's right for you, events are likely to overtake you. Others will see to it that you do what's best for *them*, and your agenda will be obliterated by theirs. If you hesitate too often, you'll be stomped on.

To manage deliberately means that you call your own shots. Ideally, this puts you ahead of the game and gives you some control over how it's played. But it also means you forego possibilities that might have opened up and been good for you.

> **To manage deliberately means that you call your own shots.**

Managing by default might feel more comfortable. Doing nothing takes no effort. But you can be sure the vacuum caused by your indecision will be filled by something. And that something is likely to hurt you.

Being deliberate does not mean that you respond to every issue with action. In fact, as we'll see, it often means that you *don't* do anything. But that's a choice, too.

Great performance is not normal

All businesses are expected to deliver growing sales and profits. There's a widespread belief that most do it as a matter of course. When management teams make forecasts, they're encouraged to aim too high and promise too much. And they happily fall into the trap.

"Stretch goals" are sexy. But consider what the FTSE100, the S&P500, or the top-ranking *Fortune* or *Forbes* companies actually deliver. The fact is, only a few of them produce more than 8 to 10 per cent growth in earnings per share for any length of time. Most do much worse, and they're shockingly erratic.

"Outperformance" is rare. Consistency is even harder to find. But macho management talk is greatly admired. That it bears little relation to reality seems to escape most people. More seriously, they miss the fact that it may have precisely the opposite effect to the one intended.

Some of your people will be sceptical when they hear, "We're aiming for 30 per cent growth in profits this year." Most are likely to give little thought to what that means. They'll nod obediently (because it's politically dumb to challenge a boss's big dreams) and go back to doing what they were doing before.

In fact, hitting such a goal is likely to be damned hard. Doing so more than once will be even harder. Without careful planning and serious effort – and probably a dose of good fortune – you'll be sure to fall short.

The lessons:
1. Be bold, but understand how rare it is for anyone to reach high numbers;
2. Think carefully about what it will take to reach your goals;
3. Commit adequate resources and focus them carefully;
4. Put processes in place that are most likely to deliver;

5. Remove roadblocks;
6. Push hard for rapid results;
7. Persevere.

Great performance may not be normal, but it is entirely *possible*. Success begins with an ambitious goal, clarity about what it'll take to get there, and skilfully applied effort. Of course, everyone knows this. Pity they don't apply it.

Attitude

The best sportspeople train hard. They have some physical gift such as size, rhythm, hand–eye coordination, or muscle structure that's appropriate to their sport. But what finally gives them their edge is their *attitude*. When everything comes down to a win-or-lose moment, they're able to hit that last great shot, sink a critical putt, or summon up an extra ounce of courage, strength, or speed.

Business conditions are always tough. Things never go the way you'd like them to for long. Every day brings new challenges, hassles, and threats. But usually there are possibilities too. There is almost always "a way out." Somewhere there's an opportunity just waiting to be exposed.

You have a lot on your plate. And you have a choice: either you can back down or buck up. You can shirk from reality, or look it in the eye and deal with it head-on. You can let circumstances determine your fate, or you can take charge.

Business is not for sissies. If you don't like it, do something else. Get on with the job, or go away. There's no point in being miserable and

Business is not for sissies. **If you don't like it, do something else.** dragging others down with you, when there's so much to do, fun to be had, and money to be made.

When your day of reckoning comes, you'll be measured by what you *did*, not by what you said or by your reasons for failing. No one will care that you knew what could *not* be done.

Winning is an attitude thing. It begins with really, really, *really* wanting to succeed. You also have to believe passionately that you can, and you have to act like a winner.

As a leader, your job is to foster these habits in your team. You are their role model. It's a big responsibility, and it takes big balls.

What you know

The stuff in your head right now can be an asset or a liability. It can be very valuable or lethal to your ambitions. It can be a catalyst for growth and change ... or a block to creativity.

What you know comes from where you've been. It's all about the past. Now, as you head into the future, you need to question it deeply. Is it still relevant? Is it still of value? Is there another way to see things?

What "you know" may be true. It may be based on irrefutable fact. But it might be no more than an assumption – you think something to be so, for whatever reason. Or it might be nothing better than a guess. Or maybe just plain *wrong*.

Let's check.

What do you know *for a fact* about:
- The environment?

- Your stakeholders (customers, competitors, suppliers, investors, employees, society, etc.)?
- Your products and services?
- Your business processes?
- The technology you use (in your offerings and your business processes)?

Now ask yourself:
- Could there be another view – and what is it?
- What does this mean to us?
- What should we do about it?

Talk to people inside your organization, who don't usually get asked these things. Talk to outsiders. Imagine you're one of them – how would that change your view?

If what you know in a week, a month, or a year is only what you know today, your outlook is bleak. But let some old thoughts out and some new ones in, and infinite possibilities await you.

What if...?

Are you trapped by what *is* – by the way things are right now? Well, what if they were different? What if you could change them? What if you:
- Involved your whole company in a huge strategic conversation?
- Tossed out your "to do" list and concentrated on doing a handful of things brilliantly?
- Abandoned one of your most profitable products today?
- Explored a market you now know nothing about?

- Decided to really "go global"?
- Outsourced some of the work you think is a core competence?
- Got out of your office and talked to 50 of your people today ... and another 50 next week ... and so on?
- Stopped advertising?
- Hired another 20 salespeople?
- Spent more of your promotional money on permission marketing?
- Got rid of some long-time customers who no longer buy as much as they used to?
- Signed for a new accounting system today?
- Fired someone who apparently has a hold on key customers, but constantly politicks and causes trouble inside your firm?

What if you kept asking, "What if...?" about everything you do?

Beginner's mind

To say that someone is "full of shit" means they're rude, difficult, or wrapped up in themselves. More truthfully, it means that they refuse to see things our way, won't agree with us, or won't change to suit us.

But why should they? They have minds of their own, after all.

Each of us is trapped by our world view – literally, our "mental tape-recording" of our past. (Terms like paradigm, mental model, and mindset mean the same thing.) We gather a lot of baggage on our journey through life. We all have our own likes and dislikes, beliefs and values, and our behaviour is shaped by this stuff.

Faced with anything new – a challenge, a threat, a problem, an argument – we respond by playing back the old tape, to see if there's anything on it that will help us. Sometimes we're lucky. Experience can be extremely valuable. (The older we are, the longer the tape is, and the more is on it. When you've "been around the block," you may be able to quickly make sense of complex issues, and avoid mistakes that a novice might make.)

Each of us is trapped by our world view – literally, our "mental tape-recording" of our past.

But experience is no guarantee of good decisions. In fact, precisely because you gained it in the past, it can get in the way of how you deal with the future. Our world views harden with time. We don't easily change our minds.

If a little knowledge is a dangerous thing, a lot can be even worse. As long as we cling to "the facts," revere our experience, and keep reliving it, we won't see "what could be."

What we "know" gets in the way of discovery. We need to empty our minds to make space for new insights. It's what Zen masters call "beginner's mind."

Repeatability

Doing something once may be easy. It can be a matter of skill or luck – or both. Doing it twice can be easier if you learned something the first time, harder if you didn't. Mastery is being able to do it again and again.

Repeatability is a valuable asset. One sale can get your business off the ground, but you need more to keep it aloft. One quality product may get early attention from customers, but you have to make lots more good ones to build your reputation. Fixing one service problem may send a customer away happy, but you have to deliver consistent satisfaction to keep customers coming back.

Although yesterday's experience can get in the way of your progress, it can also be an invaluable building block for today and tomorrow. You either use it or lose it. You have to keep asking, "What have we done today that worked? How can we do it again?" And you have to share that learning, shout from the rooftops about its value, and keep pushing for it to become embedded in "the way we do things around here."

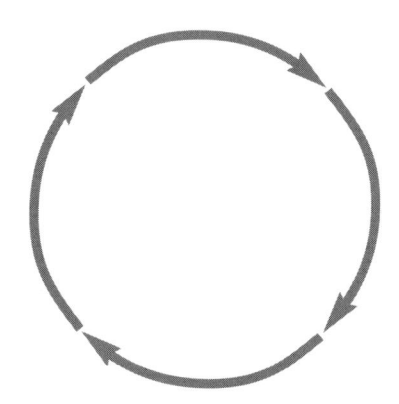

Break that pattern!

Chances are that today your company will do pretty much what it did yesterday. Is that good or bad? It depends.

The purpose of learning should never be to create a perfect solution. There's no such thing as "one best way." Learning is a process without end. Growth is only possible if new knowledge spawns more new knowledge.

The human brain is a wondrous organ. It's able to soak up an astonishing amount of information and organize it into patterns so we can make sense of what's happening around us. But the world keeps changing. A pattern that's valuable one day may be dangerous the next. If you don't consciously break those patterns, they soon cause trouble.

Your current business strategy was designed for certain conditions. It may still work for years. But pursuing it might be the very worst thing you can do. There comes a time in the life of every human being – and every organization – when you have to take a reality check.

If you decide that it's time for a change, the first challenge is to break the pattern that you're locked into. Somehow, you have to "shock the system" so that new thinking becomes possible.

One way is simply to talk about your situation. This is always important. Never underestimate the need to put facts on the table, and to confront and debate them openly and thoroughly.

But never overestimate the value of doing this, either. If you want change to happen, you have to *live* it. You have to *do* something new. You have to act. Talk is not enough.

What does this mean for your organization today? What can you do immediately to break the pattern you're in? What specific actions will change your course?

You might try:
- Changing key people on your team;
- Challenging them to radically change a key activity;
- Visiting another company, to learn from it;
- Inviting five key customers to your next strategy meeting;
- Launching a new product in half the usual time.

Companies are prisoners of their past. They learn to do things in a particular way, and just keep doing it. So almost any activity, process, or entrenched belief is a sitting duck for change.

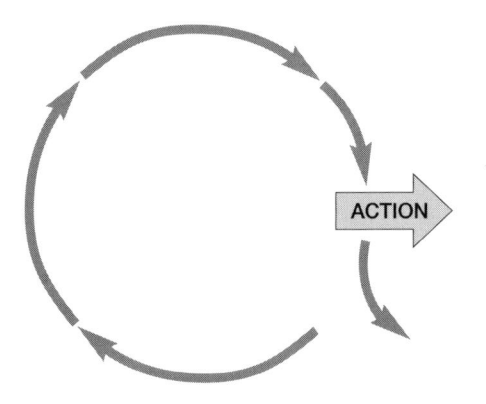

Strategy, leadership, and change

Obviously, strategy, leadership, and change management are different. Each is a specific activity, discipline, and field of study. But because everyone knows this, we overlook something that should be just as obvious:

*Strategy, leadership, and change management are all **processes**, not **events**.*

Whether you put on your strategist's hat, your leader's hat, or your change manager's hat, the work before you is fundamentally the same – *to take your organization to a different and hopefully better place.* And to do that, you have to make four things happen:

1. Create dissatisfaction with the status quo. (So people will let go of the past.)
2. Debate possible futures. (To open minds to new options.)
3. Act to learn. (To discover what actually works in the real world.)
4. Review, reflect, and revise. (To learn and adjust course … and hopefully also to drum up more dissatisfaction and thus provoke further change.)

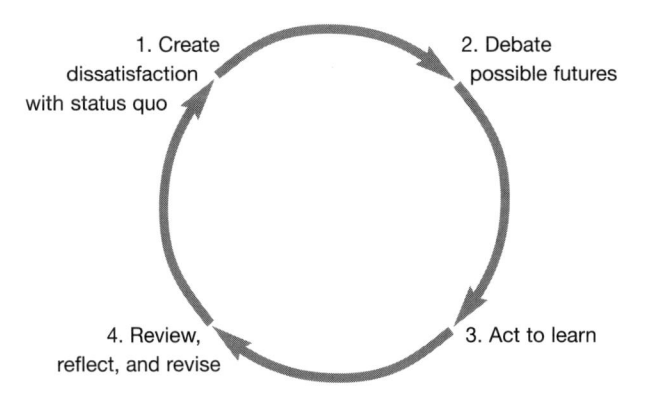

```
        1. Create                    2. Debate
     dissatisfaction              possible futures
    with status quo

     4. Review,                    3. Act to learn
   reflect, and revise
```

Strategy, leadership, and change tend to be seen as quite separate, and are treated sequentially. First, we talk strategy. Then we need a change management process to implement it. And, by the way, leadership is required to drive things.

The downside in this approach is that it separates things that shouldn't be separated.

Typically, strategic plans are created by a few people – usually members of the top team. Then "the masses" get their instructions. But why should they obey?

Implementing strategy always involves some kind of change. Telling people to change is always less effective than having them decide for themselves that change is necessary. Telling them *what* to change, and *how*, adds insult to injury and is sure to get their backs up and drive their motivation down.

Implementing strategy always involves some kind of change.

As resistance grows, it seems that the only answer is "strong leadership." So the CEO or other members of the top team step in and try to muscle things along. Mostly, this causes even more resistance, teamwork breaks down, and grand plans get derailed.

Once implementation slows, it becomes easy to forget why those plans made sense in the first place, and to dump them altogether. Instead of a *virtuous* cycle – insights, ideas, decisions, action, learning – you get a *vicious* cycle of cynicism, selfishness, excuses, and paralysis.

The best way to inspire creative thinking about your strategy and turn ideas into action is to:
1. Involve as many people as early as possible in talking about it;
2. Challenge them to suggest alternative paths to the future;
3. Urge them to act, in order to learn what works and what doesn't;
4. Help them reflect on their performance and, where necessary, adjust course.

This also happens to be the best way to trigger deep-down change. And it's the best way to lead your team to a different and better place.

Skills of the strategist

If you were to hire a strategy consultant today, you should expect him to bring four things to your business:
1. A keen understanding of the **context** in which you operate;
2. A thorough grasp of key strategy and business **concepts**;
3. Fresh **insights** about the world, your company, your customers, and your competitors – and, of course, about strategy;
4. The **judgment** to be able to tell what matters from what doesn't, to distinguish good ideas from bad, to choose the best course from among many, and to know when to act and when to wait.

Any strategist worth his salt should understand the world in which you and your competitors face off, and in which your customers make buying decisions. He should understand what's going on in your industry, and around it in politics, economics, society, and technology. He should know what trends are unfolding, and what challenges are coming down the line at you.

Second, he should be familiar with the theories of strategy and business, and of the ideas that apply specifically to *your* business. He needs to know what tools are available and which to apply, when, and how. Without a solid background, he'll probably try to shoe-horn the wrong ones into your organization. (If you only have a hammer, everything looks like a nail!)

Third, he should help you and your team see the world through new eyes. It's not enough for him to conduct research, analyse information, and produce reports. If that effort doesn't lead to a different sense of possibilities, it's a waste of time. If the outcome is not an "Aha!" revelation – "*this* is happening, *this* is what it means, *here's* how you can take advantage of it" – it's worthless.

And finally, he should be able to lay out and weigh up the pros and cons of an issue; bring logic, balance, perspective, and common sense to your discussions; and make sound decisions.

The best consultants educate you about your world, help you understand what management tools are available and which are best for you at a particular time, open your eyes – and your mind – to new opportunities, and help you lay bets with the odds in your favour. They're trend-spotters and teachers. They're analytical and creative. They provide ideas and provoke you into thinking the unthinkable. They question, inspire, challenge, coach, and motivate.

Their skill lies in knowing when to draw information and ideas out of you and your team, and when to offer a point of view that will drive conversation along a different path ... in knowing when to listen and let discussion run, and when to cut through it and change the subject. And their value rests in their ability to leave your team equipped to think about the future for themselves, and prepared mentally and emotionally to create it.

Now, if it makes sense to seek all this in a *consultant*, doesn't it make equal sense to seek it in *your own people*? Of course it does. They, too, should bring context, concepts, insights, and judgment to your organization. They run the place, after all.

So observe them carefully. Which of them has these abilities? Who is most valuable in your key meetings? Who can be developed? What must you do to develop them?

Some people are naturals: they're information junkies, they relish the cut and thrust of tough debate, and they're able to see the wood for the trees. They enjoy learning, and are blessed with the common sense to know good ideas from bad ones.

Others need help and encouragement. They have only a passing interest in the currents that might affect your company. They pay little heed to business concepts. They seldom engage in creative thinking.

You owe it to your company to identify the first type early, and make the most of them, and to develop the second crowd as fast as you can.

People learn about *context* by being curious, voracious consumers of news and opinion, and alert observers of what's going on around them. They learn about management *concepts* in a classroom, through journals and books, and sometimes through discussion with others in the know.

It's fairly easy to help them along in both areas. Enlist them in developing assumptions about your environment, so that studying their context becomes important work. Almost inevitably, they will become interested; some will become fascinated.

To develop their knowledge of management, send them on courses, and subscribe to journals like the *Harvard Business Review*, *Sloan Management Review*, *Fortune*, and *Business Week*, circulate them, and make time to talk about what's in them.

Insight and judgment are more challenging. They're products of exposure to real-world issues and involvement in "big" conversations. Whatever talents people arrive with must be honed in robust debate where they listen to competent leaders, hear a wide spectrum of views, are called on to express themselves, and are required to fight for their own ideas.

Not everyone will bring the same value to your organization. But more people will bring more value to it if you create conditions for learning and growth.

Strategic IQ

There's general agreement that emotional intelligence or EQ – what we used to call *maturity* – is a good thing in a work force. It's especially necessary in the leadership ranks where big decisions and critical judgments are made, and where the tone is set for behaviour throughout an organization.

Fortunes are spent on trying to teach EQ. Maybe this is clever. Maybe it'll work with some people. But without another kind of intelligence – *strategic* intelligence – the payoff will be limited. Balance the two, and you have a winning formula.

Strategic IQ is the ability of people to think and act strategically – to see the big picture, think long term, and take the most appropriate action now for the future. It overlaps neatly with EQ.

Like judgment, strategic intelligence is partly a natural ability, and largely learned.

With careful screening and a lot of luck, you'll probably be able to hire a few people with a high strategic IQ. They'll arrive with experience under their belts, with an understanding of your business context and of management concepts, and ready to deliver new insights that will sharpen your competitiveness. Their decision-making ability will be invaluable.

But what about the rest of your team?

Imagine if all of them – or at least a critical mass of them – could contribute in the same way. Imagine if you could rely on them to show initiative, respond instantly to issues without feeling the need to ask for permission or guidance, and act in your company's best interests. Imagine if you could trust *their* judgment as your own.

Strategic IQ is a vital element of competitiveness today, and will be even more so tomorrow. A few firms do see this, but acceptance by most is a slow, grudging process. Those firms that move fastest in taking it seriously stand to gain greatly. They'll have the edge in responsiveness, imagination, innovation, and resilience – and, above all, in *spirit*.

As with much else in management, you could leave development of strategic IQ in your company to chance. Or you could make it a matter of choice, and start working deliberately at it.

Once again, involvement in "big" strategic conversations is the key to success. Nothing beats it for making your organization really smart.

Communication

All organizations exist within an "ecosystem" of stakeholders. Those stakeholders have an interest in the success or failure of organizations, and can "vote" for or against their success. You have to manage their perceptions and expectations, or they'll make up their own minds.

Your own people are the most important audience. If they're to do the right things, they need to know what "the right things" are. Mostly, they don't.

We all know that communication is the process of sending, receiving, and interpreting messages. But what we don't know, or forget when it suits us, is that its goal is "shared meaning": in other words, that you and I both understand things the same way.

Survey after survey shows that communication is the No. 1 organizational problem and the cause of many others. Yet even when huge efforts are made to fix it, things keep going wrong and performance keeps lagging.

> Survey after survey shows that communication is the No. 1 organizational problem and the cause of many others.

One reason is that we talk *at* each other rather than *with* each other. We preach and try to convince others of our point of view. We don't invite their opinions, and we don't listen to either their ideas or their feelings.

Secondly, the wrong messages get preferential treatment. Too much importance is given to fluff and too little to substance. If a staff member has a baby or catches a fish, that's news. But facts about customers, competitors, market opportunities, and the company's priorities are tightly held by a few top people. There are too many secrets.

Third, too much communication is left to the wrong people – public relations staff (or consultants), the HR department, or secretaries. In fact, it should be the leader's work. You should be "out there" and "in your face" – evangelizing, teaching, spreading the word. This is without question your No. 1 responsibility and should be your priority.

Typically, the excuse for not doing this is, "No time." But before you say that, ask yourself, "What *is* my job?" If it's not to get results through other people, think again. If it's not to be communicator-in-chief, you haven't got the message.

Strategic conversation

Running almost any organization today is a complex matter. Many issues clutter the radar screen, and the picture keeps changing.

But the essence of what you have to do is clear. There are four central tasks:
1. Decide where to aim your team's efforts, and keep them on course;
2. Get, build, and keep necessary assets (finance, people, machines, property, customers, reputation, etc.) and capabilities (skills, processes, etc.);
3. Decide how work should be done, and apply resources so they're productive;
4. Deliver results.

While you're busy with these four activities, there are two other things you need to do in order to both facilitate and leverage them:
5. "Learn as you go," so that today's experience and knowledge become useful to your organization tomorrow;
6. Develop relationships with stakeholders (investors, staff, communities, the media, and so on) so they'll "vote" for you rather than against you.

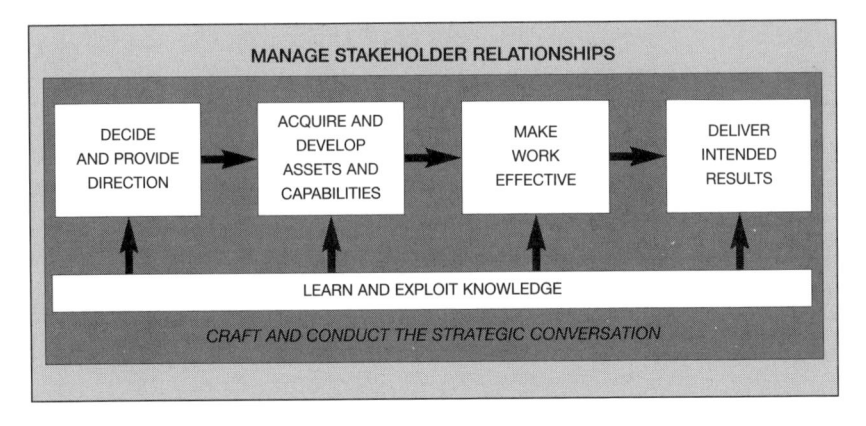

```
┌─────────────────────────────────────────────────────────────┐
│              MANAGE STAKEHOLDER RELATIONSHIPS               │
│  ┌──────────┐   ┌──────────┐   ┌──────────┐   ┌──────────┐ │
│  │  DECIDE  │→  │ ACQUIRE  │→  │   MAKE   │→  │ DELIVER  │ │
│  │   AND    │   │   AND    │   │   WORK   │   │ INTENDED │ │
│  │ PROVIDE  │   │ DEVELOP  │   │ EFFECTIVE│   │ RESULTS  │ │
│  │DIRECTION │   │ ASSETS & │   │          │   │          │ │
│  │          │   │CAPABILIT.│   │          │   │          │ │
│  └──────────┘   └──────────┘   └──────────┘   └──────────┘ │
│       ↑              ↑              ↑              ↑        │
│  ┌─────────────────────────────────────────────────────┐   │
│  │         LEARN AND EXPLOIT KNOWLEDGE                  │   │
│  └─────────────────────────────────────────────────────┘   │
│       CRAFT AND CONDUCT THE STRATEGIC CONVERSATION          │
└─────────────────────────────────────────────────────────────┘
```

There are many tools and techniques for dealing with these responsibilities. But one tool – *strategic conversation* – underpins all others. Craft and conduct it expertly, and the rest work. Do it badly, and your best intentions turn to dust.

It's easy to see that scenarios, brainstorming, six sigma quality, and performance management are all fundamentally conversational processes. But look further. The same applies to your efforts to define your core competence, develop disruptive innovations, introduce lean production, or reconfigure your supply chain. Conversation is vital in selecting customers, segmenting markets, refining your sales pitch, and briefing your ad agency.

Everything you do in business involves people talking to each other. Every meeting, every relationship, and every initiative succeeds or fails according to the conversation that takes place about them. When you acknowledge this, and when you see the potential in raising the level of conversations to make them strategic rather than merely an unnoticed fact of life, you immediately increase your ability to make an impact.

Not all conversation is strategic. A lot of it is just social interaction – and that's very important too. But what we're talking about here is:

Dialogue with a business purpose.

Strategic conversation is dialogue (two-way, take note!) that helps you hit your business goals.

Here's what it has to do:
1. Put your strategy front and centre when people meet;
2. Unclutter your corporate radar screen, explain your strategy simply and clearly, and frame it so discussions stay focused;
3. Help your people understand where they fit in, and what you expect of them;
4. Pinpoint priorities and define actions;
5. Provide pressure for results;
6. Draw out lessons, and facilitate learning;
7. Ignite the imagination and spirit of your team.

Strategic conversation may involve discussion about the environment, customers, competitors, projects, or processes – or anything else that affects your company's performance. It ensures that the right people get the right information, that they keep debates moving forward, that they have an end goal in mind, and that they seek to close the gap between talk and action.

Strategic conversation cannot be left to chance. It needs to be used deliberately, and not by default. It has to be *managed*. To make it effective, you need to consider three factors:
1. *What* to talk about (be specific, deal with high-priority issues);
2. *Who* should be involved (be sure the right people are there, and if there's a question of numbers, invite many rather than a few);
3. The *quality* of the conversation (both robust and respectful).

You can engage people in strategic conversation at almost any time – your very next meeting, a strategy retreat, or even a quick one-on-one discussion in the hallway. Every interaction offers you the chance to shape and sell your strategy. And although you should use every opportunity to do that *inside* your firm, you should also reach *outside*, to customers, competitors, and other stakeholders.

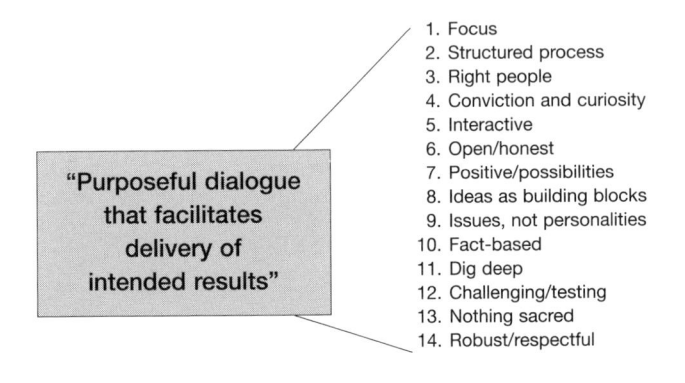

"Purposeful dialogue that facilitates delivery of intended results"

1. Focus
2. Structured process
3. Right people
4. Conviction and curiosity
5. Interactive
6. Open/honest
7. Positive/possibilities
8. Ideas as building blocks
9. Issues, not personalities
10. Fact-based
11. Dig deep
12. Challenging/testing
13. Nothing sacred
14. Robust/respectful

The ValuePlan

To make your strategic conversations effective, you need some kind of frame for them. You need to remove clutter and make your plan to create value clear and simple. You have to explain:

1. "That's where we're going" – our "hill";
2. "Here's what we must do to get there";
3. "This is what *you* must do."

Many companies use my ValuePlan framework to do this.* Unlike a balanced scorecard, which requires you to set goals for four specified areas, this tool lets *you* decide what matters to your company.

---

* Read more about ValuePlans in my book *Competing Through Value Management*, Zebra Press, 2003.

The triangle is a handy visual hook. Because it has just three corners, it forces you to think about the three critical elements of your strategy – and not 33 or 103. (Anyone can make a long list; it's far harder deciding on a short one.)

Here's how to use it:

1. Describe your business purpose – your "hill" – in the centre of the triangle;
2. Decide on the three most important things you must manage to get there – your value drivers;
3. For each of these, list the three most important goals you should aim for;
4. For each goal, list three actions.

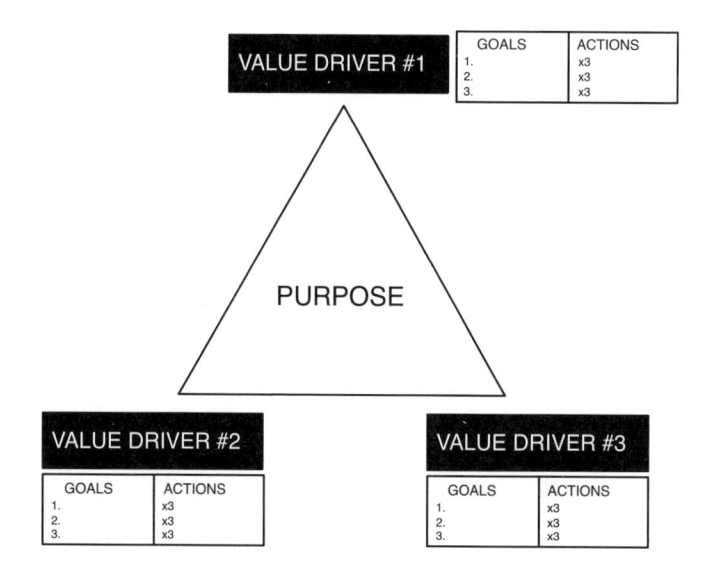

The next thing to do is to share your ValuePlan with the rest of your team, and have them break down your initial list of actions into

30-day chunks. Then, every 30 days, to review your assumptions, check your progress, and agree on new targets.

I could keep explaining. But there's really no need. This is an easy process. Don't look for reasons to make it more complicated, or harder to do. If you try, you'll be right back where you are today.

Plan to talk

There are many ways to start making strategic conversation a central factor in "how we do things around here." There's also a risk that people will laugh it off as yet another fad, and fail to take it seriously. So you need to explain its logic, make it a way of life as fast as possible, and shout about the results.

One way to start is to introduce the idea of strategic conversation into your next meeting, encourage its use, then stand back and hope the practice takes hold elsewhere. Many significant organizational changes happen like this – by "osmosis," as it were.

Another way is to start at the top and work your way down. Begin with a session where you make it clear that strategic conversation is to be an explicit process, and that you expect it to become a key practice. Highlight its use as your top team thrashes out a broad-brush strategy. Hand the strategy to a next level of divisions or departments, and once again emphasize the role of strategic conversation. Have them, in turn, pass the message on to smaller teams or individuals.

This second option is the one I prefer. Promoting the notion of strategic conversion from a high level helps embed it elsewhere. Using it demonstrates how powerful and practical it is for framing strategy and establishing priorities, and shapes the context for decisions and actions throughout your firm.

A two-day off-site meeting is the ideal forum for crafting the outline of a strategic conversation. When I'm asked to assist a client with the process, here's the agenda I propose:

1. "Making sense of strategy" – introduction to key principles, so everyone agrees on the "language";
2. Definition of key issues;
3. Definition of assumptions;
4. Development of a ValuePlan;
5. Agreement on 30-day actions.

This process is focused, and effective. Everything you need to talk about gets time. The conversation follows a logical path. You end with a shared understanding of the issues you have to deal with, the environmental challenges you face, and how you'll move ahead. You draw an easy-to-explain picture of what you aim to do – a framework for future strategic conversations. And best of all, you wind up with a handful of actions that you can drive fast.

The next step is to rapidly communicate the outcome of this meeting to other parts of your organization – most importantly, your ValuePlan and 30-day actions.

Pick your "hill"

Most vision and mission statements are fluffy things. They have zero impact on the way firms behave.

Clever people put an astonishing amount of work into writing absolute crap. They lose sight of what they need to do, and waste time wrestling over trivia – "Should we say 'excellent' or 'unbeatable'?" ... "Do we need a comma here, or should we use a dash?" ... "Does 'No. 1' sound better than 'the leader'?" They toil over insignificant detail, argue endlessly about issues that no one else will care about, and lay down words with all the passion and pain of a bestselling novelist. (And of course, the result is pure fiction!)

Vision and mission are badly misused terms. It's important to understand what they mean:

- Vision describes an organization's *ambition* – where it aims to go;
- Mission describes *what it does and how it will get where it's going.*

This isn't complicated. Yet the terms are often confused. The resulting mishmash tells no one anything useful. The words get emblazoned, engraved, recited, and repeated, often at great cost and with deep passion. They get hauled out in strategy meetings, slotted into speeches, and showed off in lifts, ads, brochures, and annual reports. All for nothing.

Fortunately, there is a better way. Instead of getting into a vision/mission bind, just try answering this question:

Why do we exist?

The answer describes your *purpose* in life. What you're here to do, what you aim to do, and what you aim to be utterly brilliant at – "That's the hill we're going to take." (And isn't that what you were trying to say with your vision and mission?)

All of us need a purpose in life. It sets our agenda. It frames our goals. It defines our activities. It gets us up in the morning, makes our efforts worthwhile, and stretches us constantly. People without purpose never reach their potential. Nor can purposeless organizations succeed.

Your purpose may be one word or a handful. Keep it as brief as you can, or you won't be able to communicate it – and you'll forget it fast, anyway. A few bullet points will do.

Once you've written it, make sure your whole team knows it. Use every possible opportunity to spell it out, explain it, and discuss it. People need to know not just what it says, but what it means. Especially what it means to them.

Your "right" customer

"Who is our customer?" is one of the first questions to ask when creating a strategy. The answer you'll get from a lot of managers is, "Everyone." But the customer is never everyone. It's always a subset or segment of all the targets available to you. If you're not tough about this decision, you'll lose every fight that follows. Inevitably, you'll lapse into "spray and pray" mode.

Instead of asking, "Who is our customer?" try asking, "Who is our *right* customer." In other words, which customer is best for your business?

Some customers are worth more to you than others. Some should be avoided at all costs.

The wrong customer	The right customer
• Takes forever to make up their mind and sign an order;	• Decides fast;
• Wants endless extra information and presentations;	• Is happy with your first pitch;
	• Accepts your price;
	• Doesn't ask for extras;
• Haggles over price;	• Doesn't complain;
• Wants lots of "extras" thrown in at no cost;	• Doesn't expect extraordinary service;
• Bitches about everything;	• Pays on time (or in advance);
• Makes unreasonable service demands;	• Speaks well of you in the marketplace;
• Doesn't pay on time;	• Is a rich source of information, insights, and ideas;
• Doesn't speak well of you in the marketplace;	• Gives you new business leads.
• Teaches you nothing.	

Today, before you do anything else, sit down with your colleagues and define your "right" customer. Consider factors like these:
- Demographics – numbers (and growth), age, sex, race, language, education;
- Purchasing power (current and potential);
- Social or work position, influence, etc.;
- Accessibility – where are they? How easy is it to get to them? How can you reach them (location of your premises, face-to-face contact, media)?;

- Cost and complexity of dealing with them;
- Image and reputation ("Do we want to be associated with these people?");
- Their attitude towards partnering you;
- Their value to you as partners.

Doing this will tell you who you should be calling on. It will also tell you who you should *avoid* – and that's not a list managers like to contemplate. But best decide that now, before you waste another cent in the wrong places.

Value

"Value" is in the eye of the person on the receiving end. What *you* think doesn't matter; all that counts is what your *customers* perceive.

You have to explain your offer, to have the best chance of convincing them. Sometimes, you'll be able to change their minds in your favour. But ultimately they decide.

No matter how passionate you are about your products and services, you won't sell them if customers don't want them. Or you might crack one sale but never another.

Satisfied customers are your most powerful marketing weapon. The more of these "missionaries" you can get on your side, the better. Unhappy ones do enormous harm. They're the talkers. And almost always, they exaggerate their moans to make a great story.

To deliver value, you first have to know what it is. Then, you have to develop the capabilities

Satisfied customers are your most powerful marketing weapon.

you need to produce it. And you have to be so good at what you do that you really make a difference that matters.

Value is a moving target. You have to keep reinventing your offering.

As customers learn what's available, learn what products and services can do, and face more choices, their expectations change. They want more and more for less and less. If you don't stay ahead of the curve, you wind up as roadkill.

Timing is everything. Being a pioneer sounds sexy, and may be good strategy. It can also be lethal, because you're likely to get lots of arrows in your back.

Being a follower can sometimes be the surest way to win. When you *respond* to customer demands, you know exactly what they want. You don't have to waste time experimenting.

But don't bank on being able to do that in time to beat your competitors. Rather, put yourself ahead of the game. Strive always to anticipate shifts in customer behaviour, and be ready to meet their new needs when it suits you.

Results that matter

If there's one word that will dominate business discussions in the future, it's "sustainability." Once this meant financial survival. Now it means much more.

New thinking about corporate governance has made the "triple bottom line" – economic, social, and environmental performance – the be-all and end-all.

In principle, this is a good thing. Companies are, after all, "citizens" of the world. We should be better off because they're there.

In practice, a business is first and foremost a "results machine." And while it must conduct its affairs in harmony with its environment and deliver value to a range of stakeholders, the first result it must produce is *profit*. It must make more money than it uses.

Companies can only do good when they do well. They have to produce profits to be able to provide jobs, contribute to the community, or pay for clean production processes. There's no free lunch.

Profit performance begins and ends with your ability to give customers more for less than your competitors can do. Get this right, and your company can be a model citizen. Get it wrong, and you'll consume resources and be a drain on all around you for as long as you survive.

Companies can only do good when they do well.

It's easy to forget this. Executives are under pressure to be do-gooders. They're expected to satisfy everyone. So you need to keep reminding yourself of your true purpose. And you need to make it clear to the people around you.

Your business will do best when your team understands that you must perform in all three areas of the triple bottom line, but that your priority is to make money. Fuzzy goals are distracting and costly.

Any number will do

Businesses have to earn more than their total cost of capital. So you need to know what you earn, and you need to know what your cost of capital is.

But how should you measure success? What number – or ratio – should you use as the target for your team? Is one better than another?

Should you worry about return on investment (ROI) ... return on equity (ROE) ... return on assets (ROA) ...?

Simple answer: it really doesn't matter. Pick one. Pick *any* one. All you need is a target to challenge your team, and against which you can track performance over time.

Focus on it like a laser. And explain to your people that no matter which overall number you choose, there are just four things they can do to change your fortunes:

1. Sell more (units of whatever you sell);
2. Increase prices;
3. Speed up your stock turnover;
4. Cut costs.

Now, set specific goals for each of these. Suddenly, what needs to be done becomes very clear. With the numbers demystified, everyone can get down to work. And you can be sure they're busy with the right things.

Define your "difference"

To reach your business potential, you have to stand out. The fact is,

> *"If you don't make a difference,*
> *you don't matter."*

Think about that. If your company doesn't make a difference that matters to me, I'll go somewhere else. There are plenty of other places for me to shop, unless you're a rare specialist – and those are getting scarcer by the minute.

So ask:

1. What is our business difference (value proposition)?
2. Why does it matter to our chosen customers?

Think about it from a personal point of view, too. If *you* don't make a difference that matters to the people around you, they'll start looking around. You'll struggle to hold their attention.

So ask:
1. What's my personal difference? (And remember, different strokes for different folks!)
2. Why does it matter? (Again, to each recipient *personally*.)

Don't be in too much of a hurry to answer these questions. Wrestle with them. Your decision here defines everything else you'll do from now on. It's the frame for your life.

Sources of advantage

Here are ten sources of competitive advantage. Become "best of breed" in one, and you'll probably do quite well. Become a star in several, and you get harder to catch.

1. The **functionality** of your product or service – what it does for customers, how, and how well;
2. The **quality** of your offering;
3. Its **price**;
4. How easy it is to **access**;
5. The **image** of both your offering and your company;
6. **Standards** such as performance, measurements, underlying technologies, compatibility, etc.;

7. The **system** it's a part of, and the extra parts, extensions, applications, etc., that are available;
8. The **service** that accompanies the sale and follows afterwards;
9. After-sales **support** (information, training, repairs, etc.);
10. The customer's total ownership **experience**.

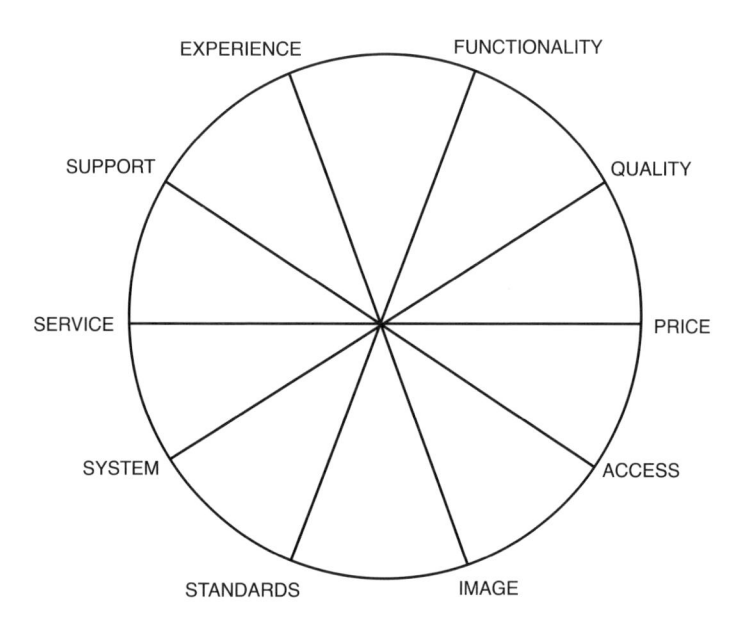

20 questions

Strategists need to ask a lot of questions. Here are 20 that you need answers to at some time or another. Maybe you've already answered some of them. Some might be particularly pertinent right now. It's up to you which you deal with – but ultimately, you do need to deal with all of them.

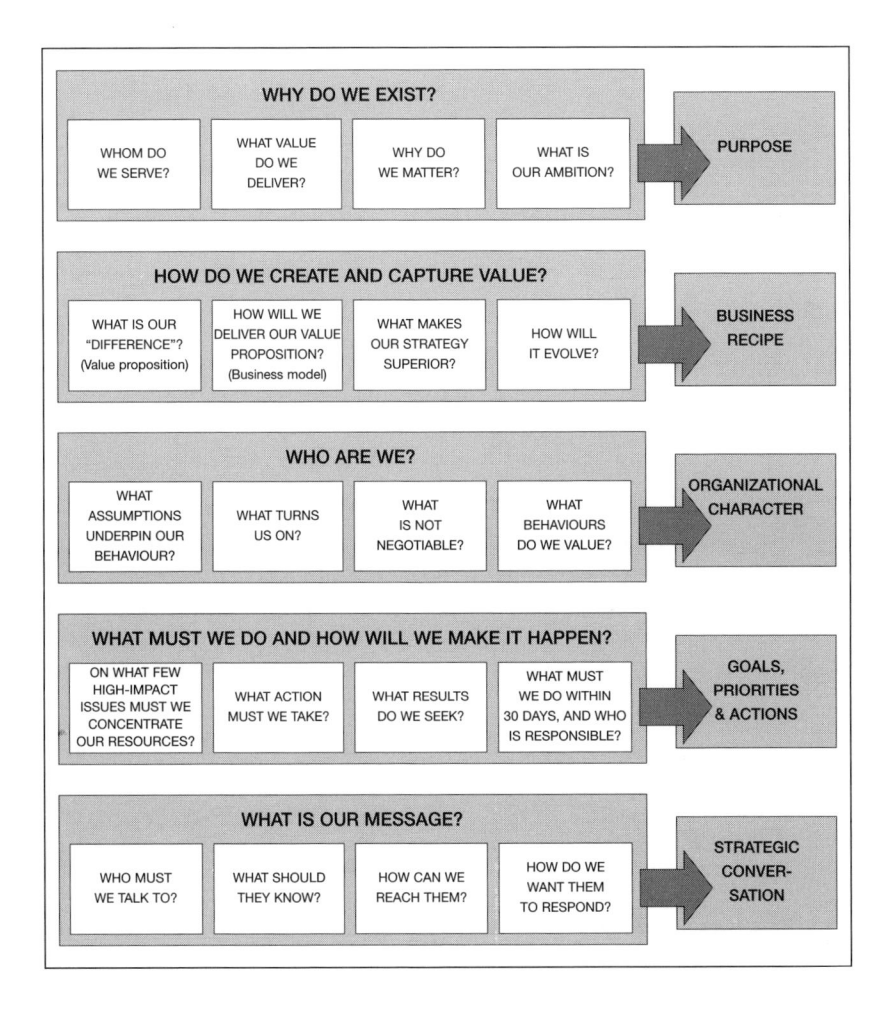

WHY DO WE EXIST?

- WHOM DO WE SERVE?
- WHAT VALUE DO WE DELIVER?
- WHY DO WE MATTER?
- WHAT IS OUR AMBITION?

→ **PURPOSE**

HOW DO WE CREATE AND CAPTURE VALUE?

- WHAT IS OUR "DIFFERENCE"? (Value proposition)
- HOW WILL WE DELIVER OUR VALUE PROPOSITION? (Business model)
- WHAT MAKES OUR STRATEGY SUPERIOR?
- HOW WILL IT EVOLVE?

→ **BUSINESS RECIPE**

WHO ARE WE?

- WHAT ASSUMPTIONS UNDERPIN OUR BEHAVIOUR?
- WHAT TURNS US ON?
- WHAT IS NOT NEGOTIABLE?
- WHAT BEHAVIOURS DO WE VALUE?

→ **ORGANIZATIONAL CHARACTER**

WHAT MUST WE DO AND HOW WILL WE MAKE IT HAPPEN?

- ON WHAT FEW HIGH-IMPACT ISSUES MUST WE CONCENTRATE OUR RESOURCES?
- WHAT ACTION MUST WE TAKE?
- WHAT RESULTS DO WE SEEK?
- WHAT MUST WE DO WITHIN 30 DAYS, AND WHO IS RESPONSIBLE?

→ **GOALS, PRIORITIES & ACTIONS**

WHAT IS OUR MESSAGE?

- WHO MUST WE TALK TO?
- WHAT SHOULD THEY KNOW?
- HOW CAN WE REACH THEM?
- HOW DO WE WANT THEM TO RESPOND?

→ **STRATEGIC CONVERSATION**

Positioning

As a strategist, you should obviously strive to be different in the eyes of customers – to position yourself apart from your competitors, and to "run a different race." But while you do that, be aware of the shortcomings in this advice:

1. There are hordes of competitors in just about every industry, and many more arriving all the time.
2. Every industry has its own "rules of the game" – and every competitor has to abide by them and master them. To sell pies, for example, you have to get certain things right. You might borrow ideas from, say, an airline or a car maker, but you have to act pretty much like other pie vendors.
3. Sooner or later – and mostly *sooner* – products and services in any category start to look alike. Price wars erupt. Every competitor joins in, and, ironically, they commoditize their own offerings.
4. To escape the sameness trap, everyone innovates. Everyone's offering improves. Customers get used to "new and improved," so they demand more of it.

Conclusion: it's extremely unlikely that you'll be able to run a different race for long. Winning may depend on *running faster than anyone else*. This means:

1. Innovating faster;
2. Adding more new advantages;
3. Being more aggressive in the marketplace.

Get the mix right, and you have a formula for a long life and lots of profits. Get it wrong, and the game is over.

You should go all-out for the very best strategy possible. But you also need to execute it brilliantly and with great perseverance.

Focus, value, costs

Every business has to abide by three principles:
1. You have to **focus** on the right customer (which means you focus on building specific internal capabilities);
2. You have to constantly improve their perception of the **value** you offer;
3. You have to relentlessly drive down your **costs**.

These are immutable laws, not nice-to-do intentions. You have to obey them to survive.

Where you focus can be decided by you or a small team. But you can't drive value up and costs down on your own. It involves everything you do, and the way you do everything. Your whole organization has to get involved. So put this picture on your walls today, and make sure every one of your people understands the message.

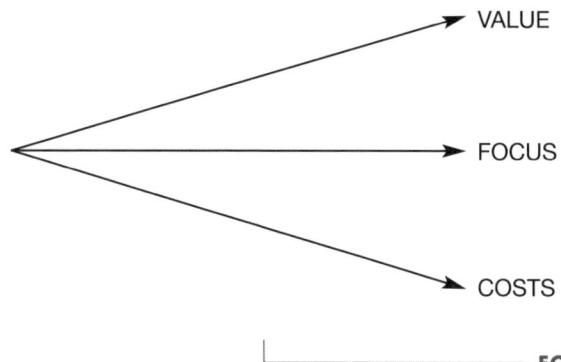

```
         ──► VALUE
   <
         ──► FOCUS
         
         ──► COSTS
```

Make your focus decision. Then, set some value and cost targets, and start your race to the future.

The "results machine"

How will you deliver the value you promise? That's the function of your "results machine" – also known as your business model. So the way you design it is central to your competitiveness.

The 7Ps framework helps you through the process by highlighting the key factors you need to think about.*

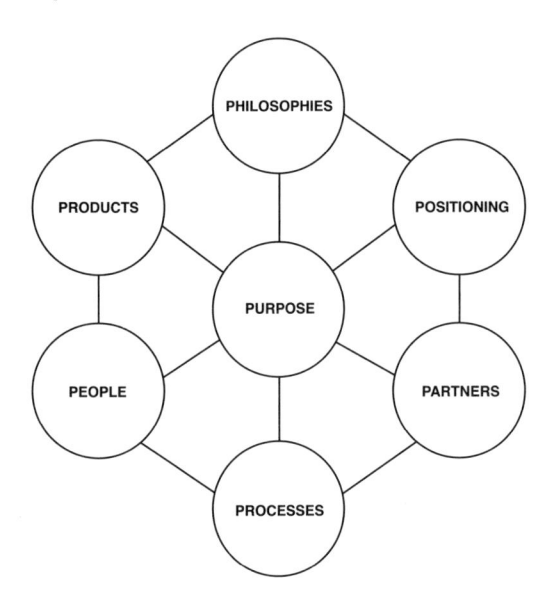

```
            PHILOSOPHIES
    PRODUCTS        POSITIONING
            PURPOSE
    PEOPLE          PARTNERS
            PROCESSES
```

---

* See Appendix 2 for a questionnaire that will help you think through the 7Ps.

Each of the "Ps" might provide an opportunity for you to gain an edge. Together, they should add up to a business recipe that meets three criteria:
1. It must deliver your value proposition to your "right" customers;
2. The elements should be tightly interconnected, so (a) they support each other, and (b) the whole thing is hard for competitors to understand or copy;
3. It should be unique.

Growth choices

It would be nice if there were an infinite number of ways to grow your business. In fact, there are just two:

> *1. Increase sales revenue from your current customers;*
> *2. Add new customers.*

Both offer a few possibilities for action (emphasis on the few!). To get more money from today's customers, you can:
1. Re-segment your current market, redefine your "right" customers,* and focus on them;
2. Re-focus resources to make the 80/20 principle work for you;
3. Add value to your offering through innovation or improvement;
4. Promote and sell more aggressively;
5. Sell "add-ons" such as accessories, complementary products or services, extended warranties, service packages, etc.;

---

* More on this on page 59

6. Cancel or reduce discounts;
7. "Unbundle" and explain your offering, and charge for all of it;
8. Increase your prices.

To capture and keep new customers, you can:
1. Pursue new market segments;
2. Expand geographically.

These are not long lists. Work through them one point at a time. You'll be sure to find new ways to pump up your sales and profits.

Opportunity search

In the good old days, business was fairly simple. Things changed quite slowly around you, and there was plenty of time to decide what to do next. You could make and sell stuff without bothering too much about service. It made sense to own every step in the production process. You could pretty well ignore what we now call "stakeholders." You could mess up the environment, and no one cared.

But look what's changed:
1. The outside world is in constant flux. Every day brings surprises. You have to detect and interpret them in real time. You also have to know about changes and developments within your organization, so you can connect what's happening inside with what's needed outside. This means you have a **sensing** role.
2. Customers are the lifeblood of business, and service is critical in the war for customers. Producing and delivering the value they want is your **serving** role.

3. Very few companies own the entire production process. Instead, they focus on their core competencies, and outsource the rest. Thanks to technology and sophisticated supply chains, you can get almost everything you need this way. Thus, **sourcing** is your third role – and an increasingly vital one.
4. You have to live in harmony with a wide range of stakeholders. Once, shareholders were the only ones managers worried about; profit was the sole measure of performance. Now, the "triple bottom line" is fashionable and you have to deliver economic, environmental, and social value. **Symbiosis** is your fourth role.
5. Today's business leader needs to be more like an orchestra conductor and less of an autocratic boss. Your job is to pull things together, to coordinate various efforts, and to apply resources where and when they're needed. This, your most important role, is about **synthesis**.

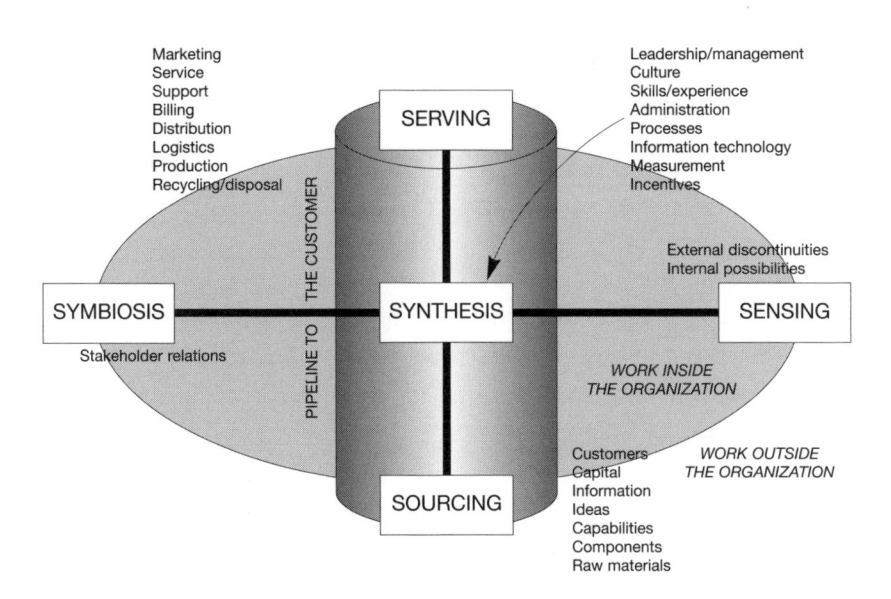

```
                    Marketing                              Leadership/management
                    Service                                Culture
                    Support                                Skills/experience
                    Billing                                Administration
                    Distribution      SERVING              Processes
                    Logistics                              Information technology
                    Production                             Measurement
                    Recycling/disposal                     Incentives

                                                           External discontinuities
                                                           Internal possibilities
       SYMBIOSIS              SYNTHESIS              SENSING
       Stakeholder relations
                                                    WORK INSIDE
                                                    THE ORGANIZATION

                                        Customers     WORK OUTSIDE
                                        Capital       THE ORGANIZATION
                                        Information
                              SOURCING  Ideas
                                        Capabilities
                                        Components
                                        Raw materials
```

(Vertical axis: PIPELINE TO THE CUSTOMER)

The 5Ss model can be used by any company in any industry. It's as useful to manufacturers as to service providers.

Thinking about these five roles gives you a new way to think about how to deliver maximum performance. It helps you:

1. Identify areas for innovation and improvement;
2. Reconfigure your value-creation processes;
3. Decide what work to do inside your organization, and what to assign outside;
4. Determine your priorities.

> Today's business leader needs to be more like an orchestra conductor and less of an autocratic boss.

Most importantly, it highlights the need to *integrate* activities – and to build the skills and systems you need to do that.*

Let's talk about people

The biggest challenge to business this century will be the same one that has dogged managers down the ages:

How to get results through people?

To many executives, the ideal world would be one in which people played little or no part. A company of machines would be free of politics. You wouldn't have to worry about pay scales or safety or strikes. There would be no squabbling, goofing off, deceit, or hands in the till. A happy place, indeed!

An old joke says that the factory of the future will be run by just one man and a dog. The man's job will be to feed the dog; the dog's job will be to bite the man if he touches a machine.

---

* The questionnaire in Appendix 1 will guide you in a powerful strategic conversation.

Some factories are almost people-free. Many others – and many service businesses, too – are shedding jobs fast and investing heavily in technology. But no company can get rid of everyone. Sooner or later you get down to Joe, Renée, Mandla, Mohammed, or Chan – and you're in their hands.

Business performance is the product of human imagination and spirit. Whizzy new technologies are great enablers, but on their own they deliver nothing. People always have been – and will remain – the most important resource.

Perhaps it's time, then, to stop hiding this very basic fact under clouds of bullshit.

- Start talking about "people" ... and not "human resources" – or even worse, "human capital";
- Start treating people as if they had real worth, minds of their own, and a need for meaning in their lives;
- Start showing respect for their beliefs, opinions, and ideas;
- Start honouring them by talking straight, telling the truth, and being polite;
- Start doing whatever it takes to help them reach their potential.

Motherhood, you say? Platitudes that have no place in this dog-eat-dog world, when you're under growing pressure to cut costs and boost productivity? Silly bleating from soft HR "practitioners"?

Far from it. Managers talk a great people story, but don't live it. But if they fool themselves, they fool no one else.

No business is a social club. But all businesses are *societies*. All businesses depend on social interactions to get things done. All businesses are arenas in which individuals fly ... or flounder.

No business is a social club. But all businesses are *societies*. All businesses depend on social interactions to get things done.

The end of the twentieth century saw technology take a big hit. Now it's recovering and executives are once again excited about what it might do for them. They're testing new business models and reconfiguring their organizations. Forecasters see a steady rise in IT investment in the years ahead.

You'd be a fool not to use the very best technology you can afford. But you'd be a bigger fool not to put people first. Relationships are the glue that holds things together.

What does all this mean?

- Hire the best people you can;
- Use careful induction to help them fit in, and to explain your strategy, your expectations, and their roles;
- Train and develop them constantly;
- Involve them in "big" conversations;
- Make it easy for them to share ideas;
- Give them space to figure out for themselves how to support your strategy;
- Treat them with respect and compassion;
- Hold them to account.

This time, really *do* it!

Strategic horizons

One question managers often ask is, "How far ahead should I plan?"

In the 1960s, "long-range planning" was all the rage and five- and ten-year horizons became common. In the 1980s, word spread that Japanese companies took an even longer view (Matsushita's was said to be 250 years!). And since Japanese firms were gobbling up market share in many industries and "Japanese management" was all the rage, managers in the West started talking admiringly of such vision.

But that was then and this is now.

After a couple of decades of shocks and volatility, managers have at last accepted that they can't see the future, that they will be surprised, and that acting without "all the facts" is mostly what they have to do.

Most importantly, they've woken up to the fact that the long term begins in the short term. That the future begins with the very next step you take ... or *don't* take. And that action deferred can turn grand dreams into nightmares.

Getting to the future is like eating the proverbial elephant: the only way is one bite at a time. And you have to start right now.

But you also need a sense of where you're headed. For with no clear purpose, you'll zig and zag aimlessly. Speed will just get you to the wrong place faster.

You also need to consider your industry's "clockspeed." Every sector has its own "pulse," rhythms, and cycles. Things move rapidly in the consumer electronics business and far more slowly in building materials, mechanical handling equipment, or airlines.

The pressure for change originates in different places. In industries such as pharmaceuticals or financial services, it comes largely from the inside. Soft drinks and fashion are far more sensitive to the whims of customers.

Some companies have to look 20 or 30 years ahead because they have to make massive investments with distant returns. For most, three to five years seems about right as a planning period, with the focus on year one.

Choosing the appropriate time horizon is very important. You need to decide what's best for your business. If you focus too far ahead you may overlook or underplay critical short-term issues. But if you fixate on the immediate future you may not see long-term possibilities.

Threats, challenges, and opportunities come into view at various times. The earlier you sense them, the better. But deciding just when to explore them in detail, or when to act on them, calls for careful judgment. Too soon can be pointless; too late may be perilous.

Some issues will appear on your radar screen in clear focus. Most will be a blur for longer than you'd like. How much detail you need depends on three things:

1. The lead time for change;
2. The size of your investment;
3. The reversibility of your decision.

If you need lots of time to implement a new strategy, if there's a high cost to it, and if it will be hard to walk away from, then you need plenty of preparation time. On the other hand, if you can make your new move quickly and cheaply, and if you can easily escape it, then a shorter horizon makes sense.

> *Look as far ahead as you need to and only make commitments when you have to.*

Creating tomorrow today

As a strategist, you have to act today in order to shape tomorrow. And you have to do it knowing that:

- Almost all of your decisions will be based on incomplete information;
- The impact of your choices will be felt for a long time;

- As things play out, circumstances will keep changing and new factors will come into play;
- Goalposts will be shifted.

Business decisions bounce off each other like balls on a crowded pool table. Disturb one pattern, and you may get another that you like less. A calculated tactic can quickly trigger a haphazard mess. What seems to be a clever competitive move can set your competitors up for victory. (*"What kind of idiot would want a job like this?" you might well ask!*)

Like it or not, however, you have to manage in the present for the future. You have to make sacrifices today for tomorrow. You have to take chances and make investments in hope of a payoff at a time you can't see.

This is the work of leaders. Your ability and your willingness to do it will determine your legacy. Skill and judgment are key factors. Courage matters even more.

The constant challenge is to balance today's costs and benefits with tomorrow's. You're most likely to be successful if you:

1. Think about everything you do in terms of its future impact;
2. Inform stakeholders about what you intend, and why;
3. Consider carefully how you might be surprised;
4. Assess the risks, and plan to deal with them;
5. Push hard for results in *every* period, starting right now.

Embracing paradox

It's tempting in business to take an either-or view of things because that seemingly makes them easier to understand. But life has shades of grey everywhere. Things see-saw this way and that. There are paradoxes all around us.

You have to find the happy medium between:
- The future ... and the past;
- Making profits ... but doing many things that eat into your ability to do it;
- Driving value up ... and costs down;
- Being tough ... and compassionate;
- Being bold ... and being careful;
- Taking risks ... and managing risks;
- Continuity ... and change;
- Preserving what worked yesterday ... and inventing what you need to do tomorrow;
- Controlling costs ... and investing boldly;
- Innovation ... and improvement;
- Keeping a firm grip on things ... and letting go;
- Centralization ... and decentralization;
- Having a strong point of view ... and allowing others to express their views.

This could be a much longer list. But you get the point.

It's not smart to say, "Make up your mind: what exactly do you want me to do?" For one thing, you often just won't be able to make neat choices. (Paradoxically, you have to make trade-offs to be successful, but you also have to satisfy multiple stakeholders!) For another, either-or thinking shuts out the potential of "*and*" – as in "Let's do this *and* that." And this is a sure way of narrowing your options.

```
                        OR ...
DO THIS  <----------------------------------->  DO THIS
                        AND ...
```

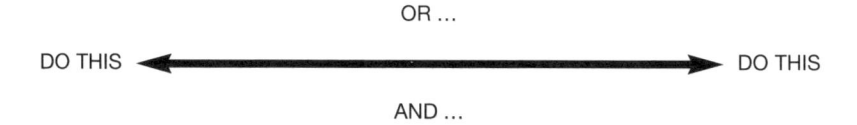

Paradoxes come at us all the time, and from every quarter. You have to deal with many of them reactively, as they arrive. But you can also use them *proactively*, as a powerful tool for identifying opportunities.

Begin by listing the paradoxes you face right now. Then rank them according to the impact they have on your business. Finally, involve your team in thinking about how to embrace them – to "do this *and* that" at the same time.

Paradoxes we face	Possibilities

This can have a profound impact on your performance. For if you manage to get your arms around tricky paradoxes while your competitors are befuddled by them, you obviously gain the edge.

Paradoxes can thoroughly confuse an organization. Or they can be a powerful competitive weapon. You choose.

Frame your view

If you've ever taken part in a business school case discussion, you'll know there are many ways to skin a cat. Almost everyone has their own take on the situation described in the case. They differ about what the key issues are, they analyse situations differently, and they disagree about what actions should follow. Where one sees a dilemma, another overlooks it or sees an opportunity. Where one fingers a senior manager as the problem, a second says the supply chain needs to be reconfigured, and a third takes aim at the competition.

In a theoretical setting, it's fun and instructive arguing about what's "right." In the maelstrom of business, robust conversation is equally valuable. Controversy and strong feelings are grist to the strategy-making mill. But you can allow people to debate and disagree for only so long. You can't keep going in circles, chewing over the same issues with no conclusion.

Leaders need to canvass a wide range of opinion and consider many views. But they also have to narrow the options before them to ensure that decisions get made. They have to make clear: "This is up for further discussion, but that is not" … "We need to focus here, not there" … "Let's talk about sales training, not about discounts" … and so on.

The challenge always is to frame things in a way that makes sense to you and to others. To choose what you will attend to and what you will ignore. And to decide on priorities – what to do first, second, third.

When possible, you should explain your reasoning. Sometimes you won't be able to, or there won't be time, and you just have to give an order.

Thinking about the future

Throughout history, humans have been fascinated by the future. Understanding what's out there has kept a lot of people busy for a long time, but with poor results. We've tried tea leaves, tarot cards, crystal balls, and computer simulations. Wise men and witches have had a go. And still, surprises keep coming.

The method has not been invented that will give you perfect foresight.

No matter how much information you gather, no matter how many smart people you put to work interpreting it, and no matter how many computers you have to crunch numbers, detect patterns, spit out possibilities, and weigh up probabilities, you *will* be caught with your pants down. Things will seldom pan out exactly as you expect. The future will unfold in the manner and time of its own choosing – and always in unforeseeable ways.

You can't avoid thinking about the future – because that's where you're headed. You might not be keen to look ahead because you can't see enough of what's out there. Or if you can, you might not like the view. But this doesn't let you off the hook.

There are basically three ways to go forward:

1. Lay your bets on a single view of the future;
2. Anticipate a range of, say, two or three different futures, describe them as well as you can, and develop plans for each;
3. Prepare to deal with whatever comes by readying people for change, and making your organization as flexible as possible.

> **The future will unfold in the manner and time of its own choosing – and always in unforeseeable ways.**

All these options are risky. The future you imagine is very unlikely to be the one that actually emerges. The more precise you are about your expectations, the greater your chances of missing the boat.

Scenario experts claim they have the answer. Don't just consider *one* future, they advise, but instead allow for *a range of possible futures*. Write stories about them. This way, you'll take your mind for a stroll, engage in some mental practice in dealing with various outcomes, and so prepare yourself for whatever actually happens. (So when tomorrow arrives, you've "been there, done that, got the T-shirt.")

It's a seductive pitch, so scenario planning has its fans. Almost every management team I know talks about "looking at some scenarios" – even though they know nothing about the technique, and actually just mean that they should chat about some trends!

What's usually ignored, however, is that the value in scenarios lies largely in the *conversation that shapes them* – and only partly in the final product. Being part of a scenario team may open your mind. Listening to a presentation or reading a report is less likely to do it. Yet more often than not, the development of scenarios is assigned to small teams. The larger organization only gets to hear about the conversation after it's over – and then gets only the bullet points.

The downside to contemplating various scenarios is *that you usually cannot escape the need to bet on a specific outcome*. "Keeping your options open" is a fine idea, but seldom a real possibility.

> *You can imagine any number of futures,*
> *but you can't bet on all of them.*

Say you develop two scenarios. One says "Do A, B, and C, and X will happen." The second says, "Do D, E, and F, and Y will happen." Now what? Do you do one or the other? Both? Or bits of both? You have to decide.

Then, what happens if parts of one scenario "leak" into the other? If, for example, the economic outlook you saw in Scenario 1 actually occurs in Scenario 2? Or if the social outlook envisaged in Scenario 2 unfolds in Scenario 1? Short answer: you're stuffed.

Some companies have to look far out into the future and lay enormous bets with little or no prospect of reversing them. Their long time horizon means they have to make lots of assumptions about what might occur, and go with one view or another. And once they start committing, they're stuck.

For example, you can't suddenly convert an aluminium smelter to a toy factory, or shift it to another location. Equally, when you sink a mine shaft, set up an oil refinery, or open a new car factory, you can't suddenly change your mind – at least, not without serious cost. So at best, considering different scenarios ensures that managers in these firms don't overlook key issues before putting down any money. It may also give them comfort that they can weather even the worst scenarios.

Other companies – in fashion, software, or speciality foods – have it easier. They can not only take a short-term view, but also hedge their bets by making numerous low-cost commitments. If something goes wrong in one area – or surprisingly *right* – they can quickly shift resources. So to them, too, scenarios are of limited help.

Forecasting by any means has a lousy track record. There is no risk-free path to the future. You may gather a lot of facts and opinions, but ultimately you have to make *assumptions* about what they mean. You can make a Plan A, plus a Plan B and a Plan C – all the way to Z – but you have to back one of them. The "ten-buck test" is ever-present.

Assumptions are the bedrock of all forecasting methods. Developing a set of shared assumptions with your team ensures that when you talk strategy, you all approach it from the same starting point. When you have them on paper, you can decide whether to build scenarios. But before you go that far, ask if doing so will make you any wiser. Chances are it won't.

Forecasting is dodgy, so while you take your best stab at it, you should also do what you can to build a resilient organization – one that can withstand trouble, and rapidly adapt to new circumstances. Here's how:

1. Raise the strategic IQ of your organization;
2. Develop habits of alertness and curiosity;
3. Constantly monitor what's happening around you, and think about what it means today and may mean tomorrow;
4. Involve as many of your people as possible as your "eyes and ears"; engage them in thinking, "What if...?";
5. Dig deep for the underlying truth;
6. Shed costs; stay "lean and mean";
7. Make your organization as flexible as possible by outsourcing all non-core activities.

Now, here are two frameworks to help you think about your business arena.

The first focuses on competition within your industry. Use it to weigh up whether you want to play, whether you *can*, what you'll be up against, and whether you'll get what you want.

The second framework encourages a wider view. As you think through it, keep asking:

- What's happening now ... and what's likely to happen?
- How might things change?
- How could *we* change them?
- What must we deal with ... and what can we ignore?

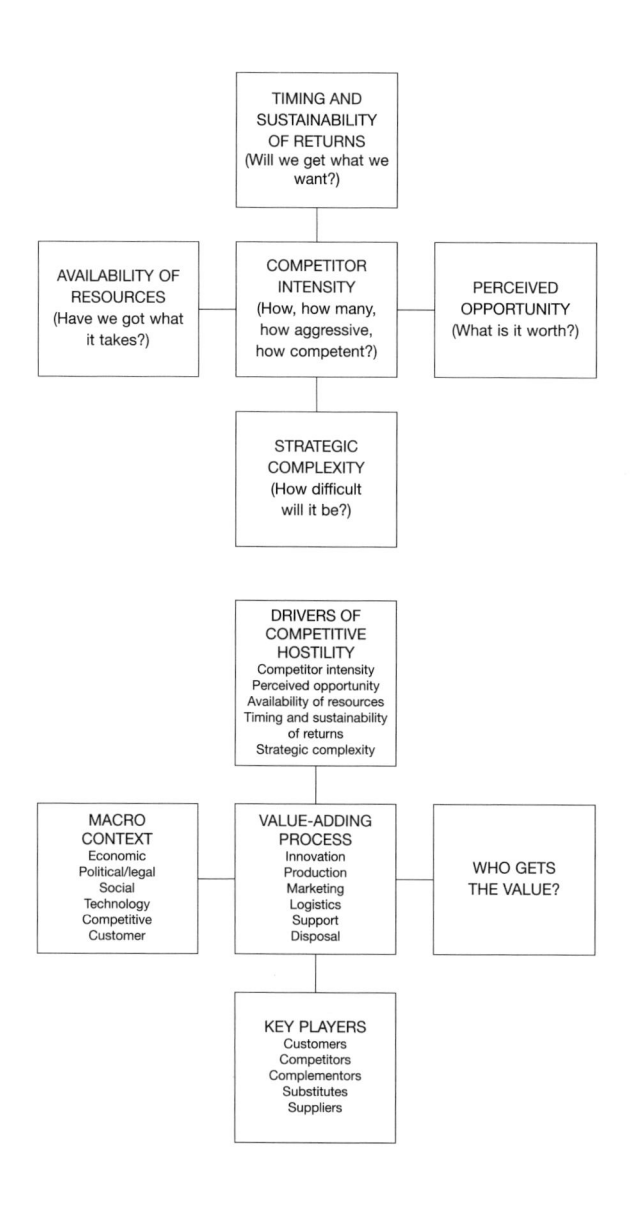

```
                    ┌─────────────────────┐
                    │  TIMING AND         │
                    │  SUSTAINABILITY     │
                    │  OF RETURNS         │
                    │ (Will we get what we│
                    │       want?)        │
                    └──────────┬──────────┘
                               │
┌──────────────────┐  ┌────────┴────────┐  ┌──────────────────┐
│  AVAILABILITY OF │  │   COMPETITOR    │  │    PERCEIVED     │
│    RESOURCES     │──│    INTENSITY    │──│   OPPORTUNITY    │
│ (Have we got what│  │ (How, how many, │  │(What is it worth?)│
│    it takes?)    │  │  how aggressive,│  │                  │
│                  │  │ how competent?) │  │                  │
└──────────────────┘  └────────┬────────┘  └──────────────────┘
                               │
                     ┌─────────┴─────────┐
                     │    STRATEGIC      │
                     │    COMPLEXITY     │
                     │  (How difficult   │
                     │    will it be?)   │
                     └───────────────────┘
```

```
                    ┌──────────────────────────┐
                    │  DRIVERS OF              │
                    │  COMPETITIVE             │
                    │  HOSTILITY               │
                    │  Competitor intensity    │
                    │  Perceived opportunity   │
                    │  Availability of resources│
                    │  Timing and sustainability│
                    │       of returns         │
                    │  Strategic complexity    │
                    └──────────────────────────┘

┌──────────────────┐  ┌──────────────────┐  ┌──────────────────┐
│     MACRO        │  │  VALUE-ADDING    │  │                  │
│    CONTEXT       │  │    PROCESS       │  │                  │
│    Economic      │  │   Innovation     │  │    WHO GETS      │
│  Political/legal │──│   Production     │──│    THE VALUE?    │
│     Social       │  │    Marketing     │  │                  │
│   Technology     │  │    Logistics     │  │                  │
│   Competitive    │  │    Support       │  │                  │
│    Customer      │  │    Disposal      │  │                  │
└──────────────────┘  └────────┬─────────┘  └──────────────────┘
                               │
                     ┌─────────┴─────────┐
                     │   KEY PLAYERS     │
                     │    Customers      │
                     │    Competitors    │
                     │   Complementors   │
                     │    Substitutes    │
                     │    Suppliers      │
                     └───────────────────┘
```

THINKING ABOUT THE FUTURE 87

Together, these frameworks give you a "fine-grained" picture of why the level of competition is where it is, what forces are at work to change things – and where there might be opportunities for you to gain an advantage.

Defining assumptions about the future deserves more attention than most management teams give the process. It should take the bulk of the time in any strategy workshop. If you do it thoroughly, you'll gain many insights. If you try to skate through it, you'll do your planning in the dark.

The future is an interesting place. There's a lot of fascinating stuff to talk about, and we all have opinions. So encourage your people to open their minds and take a broad view of the landscape. But remember, this is not a general knowledge game. As you list assumptions, *be sure to focus on what affects your company specifically*. Home in on trends that have implications for your business, not for everyone and his dog.

The "five whys"

Faced with challenges, and under pressure to get results, most of us push to get to answers instead of insights. Instead of probing past what's superficial and obvious so we can understand what's really at issue, we race off in the wrong direction to decide *what* to do, and *how*.

> Most of us push to get to answers instead of insights.

Japanese managers have long known the importance of getting to the root of issues before you try to deal with them. They use a simple technique called the "five whys" to dig deep for insights. They ask, "Why?" followed by "Why?" ... "Why?" ... "Why?" ... "Why?"

Try it in a meeting today. Whether you're talking

strategy, service, production, or anything else, the effect is likely to be the same. Some people will be irritated. Some may think you've lost it. You might feel stupid. But everyone will wind up knowing more.

Fit to fight

If your firm is in poor shape, you'll find it hard to compete with anyone worth taking on. Whatever customers you have now will be at risk. New customers will be hard to get – and harder to keep. Your profits will shrivel.

In short, your business has no future.

The laws of nature apply to companies. "Survival of the fittest" is the way things work. If there's not a good reason for stakeholders to let you stay in business, they won't. You need great product or service offerings, "best-of-breed" productivity, adequate margins, and repeat sales to generate the strong cash flows and profits that will keep you going.

There's space in most industries for numerous players. Usually, though, just two of them take most of the spoils. The rest squabble over the scraps.

You may be quite content to be one of the also-rans. You might be perfectly comfortable trailing along, picking up a few sales here and there. And you may have modest profit ambitions. But beware! You're playing a dangerous game.

Complacency is dumb when the leaders in your industry are moving and improving aggressively. The fiercer their fight, the faster and higher they'll raise standards – and the quicker you'll fall even further behind.

Newcomers will enter the fray and you'll be shoved out faster than you imagine.

Your company's health won't be improved by one stab at cutting costs, changing the culture, or improving quality. You have to work at it every day. And you have to keep working at it, year after year.

To get into good shape personally, you need to balance physical exercise with a new mental approach to life. It's the same with your company.

"Muscle-building" removes flab and waste, and builds strength. To start your programme, consider:

1. What's our goal? – the value we want to deliver, the customers we aim for, sales, profits, etc.;
2. What do we need? – plant and equipment, systems, structures, people, etc.;
3. What must we start doing? – activities, processes, serving "right" customers, etc.;
4. What must we do more of? – focus, shorter meetings, tighter deadlines, training and development, etc.;
5. What don't we need? – plant and equipment, systems, structures, people, etc.;
6. What must we stop doing? – activities, processes, serving "wrong" customers, etc.;
7. What must we do less of? – wasting time, politicking, etc.

While you shape up "physically," get to work on your company's "mental" health, too.

- Raise your sights by setting new goals, aiming at new markets, and encouraging your team to "find a better way, every day."
- Forbid toxic conversations.
- Talk possibilities, not impossibilities.

- Foster an aggressive quest for new ideas. Engage as many people as you can in robust strategic conversation.

A simple switch to talking things up, not down, can have a magical impact on performance. But competitiveness does not just come from "happy talk." If you're serious, you have to take hard decisions about every aspect of your results machine. And you should do it fast, because delay just keeps you from getting up to speed and sends a sorry signal about your commitment.

Strategy and spirit

Getting fit to fight is hard work. Every guru has a plan. But strip away the fads and the formulas, and you get down to two requirements:
1. Strategy;
2. Spirit.

Of course, you need a strategy. It must be carefully thought through, and all your people must understand it. But that's not enough. Your strategy must be underpinned and driven by a killer *spirit*. Your people must *want* to win. They must be willing to do whatever that takes. They must work hard, move fast, adapt whenever it's necessary – and keep going when the going gets really rough.

Strategy demands *thinking* skills. Fostering a competitive spirit demands *people* skills. Put the two together, and you have a winning combination.

I know plenty of top executives who're proud of their ability to shape strategy – and rightly so. But

Your strategy must be underpinned and driven by a killer *spirit*. Your people must *want* to win.

when it comes to igniting the spirit of their people, they're hopeless. They are their own worst enemies because they think that *making* strategy is everything. In fact, it's just one aspect of a complex process.

Speed

Speed is probably the most underestimated "tool" of all. But imagine the impact on your bottom line if you cut by 50 per cent the time it takes to:

- Develop new products and get them to market;
- Run a meeting, write a letter, or make a decision;
- Develop a new promotional campaign;
- Train people;
- Manufacture a product;
- Close a sale;
- Deliver your products and services;
- Complete service calls;
- Collect money from your debtors.

Strangely, doing things fast doesn't mean doing them badly. For one thing, the pressure to "do it right the first time" means you have to focus. Secondly, you have to use the most efficient methods. And third, you can't be sloppy.

With speed as a goal, you have to sharpen processes and eliminate anything that might cause friction or be a roadblock. You have to fight inefficiency, waste, and mistakes.

Cut the time it takes to do everything. Before you do anything, ask:

- Should I do this at all?
- Is there a better way?
- How can I do it faster?

Now, you might think a 50 per cent improvement is too much. But most things can be done much faster than you think. So start at 50 per cent ... and work your way up from there!

Budgeting games

Goal-setting and "gaming" go hand in hand. When budget time comes around, the CEO asks for a big number. The team tries to talk him down. To justify their position, they offer modest sales forecasts while complaining about tough business conditions. They inflate their costs. And of course, they tuck away whatever cash they can, so that come the end of the year they can "hit their numbers."

Year after year, the same thing happens in most firms. The increasing popularity of performance-based compensation ensures that this will continue.

But there is a better way.

From where you sit today, it's hard to know whether you can grow your profits by 10 per cent this year or by 20 per cent. Whatever number you pick has to be based on assumptions about the future. So you only know *after the event* what was reasonable. If the economy turns south, 5 per cent growth might be outstanding; if it takes off and customers go on a spending spree, 50 per cent might be a cinch.

A year from now, though, you'll know just how well you did given the conditions you faced. You'll also know how your competitors fared. You'll be able to make an objective assessment of how you've performed against the environment, and against them.

By pinning rewards to future performance that's little more than a guess, companies ensure that their people will fool around. But base them on *hindsight* and you do away with this silliness.

Let your team set their own bold growth targets. Goad them into aiming beyond what seems possible. Inspire them to work like fury to deliver the results. And reward people who beat the world, not the numbers.

> **Reward people who beat the world, not the numbers.**

Your aim should be to improve performance, change behaviour, and develop trust. Your people should realize that there's no need to fool with the numbers, and that if they set ambitious targets and miss them they won't be punished.

In time, budgeting will become more fun. You and your colleagues will learn to trust each other. You'll unleash energy that you never imagined was there. And the silly games will end.

Structure

On our own, any of us can do just so much. But work with someone else, and remarkable things happen. Just one partner can make a huge difference. A group of seven people is likely to achieve more than three or five.

There's strength in numbers. They give you more capacity to handle things, and more *brainpower*. And when people bat ideas back and forth, challenge each other's views, test assumptions, and build on what they've just heard or seen, a powerful multiplier effect takes hold.

All organizations start small. But if they fail to grow physically, there's a limit to how far they can grow their sales or profits. They just never benefit from the synergies that arise from shared ideas or from spreading the workload.

1+1 > 2

But this doesn't mean you have to employ more people or own more offices and factories.

Thanks to information technology, you can "atomize" your organization and locate bits of it wherever it makes most sense. Almost any capability you need can reside almost anywhere. You can contract out almost any work.

You might put a design centre in California, a research team in Geneva, or a pilot manufacturing plant in Tokyo. Your best thinkers can work in your office, from their homes in Johannesburg, or on a beach in the Seychelles. Outsiders can be tapped to test "beta" versions of your latest software, invent new biotech treatments, supply computer mother boards, or assemble your cameras, watches, or cars.

Today, big organizations can be physically quite small, and small organizations can quite easily gain many of the advantages that used to be the preserve of big ones. So now, as never before, you can be selective about who does what. You can choose what to be expert in, and which experts you need for everything else.

Managing these new work arrangements introduces new levels of complexity into organizations. Exceptional results don't come just because you focus on your core competences or enter into exciting supplier alliances. You have to put in place the factors that underpin and inspire great performance.

> **Today, big organizations can be physically quite small, and small organizations can quite easily gain many of the advantages that used to be the preserve of big ones.**

It goes without saying that strategy, people, systems, and processes are all important. But keep in mind that your *fundamental challenge is to enable people to talk to each other*. So you need to foster a conversation that gets their creative juices flowing and lets them coordinate their activities. You also need to systematically capture their ideas and catalogue, redistribute, fine-tune, and apply them.

IT is central in all this. But be clear what you should expect from it. For all its whiz-bang promise, its fundamental value is that it *facilitates strategic conversation*. It makes *people* productive by hooking them up to each other, giving them easy access to knowledge, and providing an important means of managing organizational memory.

Your strategy is only as good as your results machine makes it. Imagine that, right now, you have a blank slate and can design that machine any way you like. What will it look like?

Begin with four questions:
1. What skills do you need?
2. Who should provide them?
3. Where should they be located?
4. How will you enable the strategic conversation that will make them productive?

Design for performance

As far back as anyone can tell, organizations were pyramid-shaped, with the leader at the top and the minions at the bottom. Then, in the early 1980s, some far-seeing executives started talking about turning their organizations upside down, with customers at the top and the leader at the bottom, in a supporting role.

CEOs starting making pious speeches about "servant leadership." The notion of "intellectual capital" took off faster than you could say "dot-com." Consultants advised their clients to become "customer-centric" and invented costly ways of helping make it happen.

From being a necessary hassle, people suddenly moved front and centre in conversations about management. Customers seemed to matter. If you attended a management conference or read the latest books and articles, you'd think that something had really changed.

In fact, the rhetoric ran ahead of the reality. For all the talk that "people make the difference," a lot of organizational arrangements seem designed to *stop* them from doing that – or at least to slow them down. And customers still get short shrift.

An organization chart is little more than a drawing of what you want people to imagine. It's a mental map of who's who in the zoo, who has power, and who reports to whom. And as long as it *looks* like a pyramid, people will act as though the "best and the brightest" are at the top of the pile and the rest are down where the work gets done.

An organization chart is little more than a drawing of what you want people to imagine.

Chartists use various conventions to make sure no one misunderstands anything. Your value, role, and influence are signalled by where you fit on the "organogram." They're defined by the size of the box that has your name in it (code for offices, cars, and perks), and whether you're linked to other people by solid lines or dotted ones. If you get a big box at the top, you matter. If you're lower down ... well, tough.

Because of this, it makes huge sense to want to "climb the ladder." Ambition is a powerful motivator, so it's a good thing that people aspire to advance. The trouble is, power may go to their heads. They may lose perspective and become puffed up with their own importance. When that happens, position easily becomes more important than contribution.

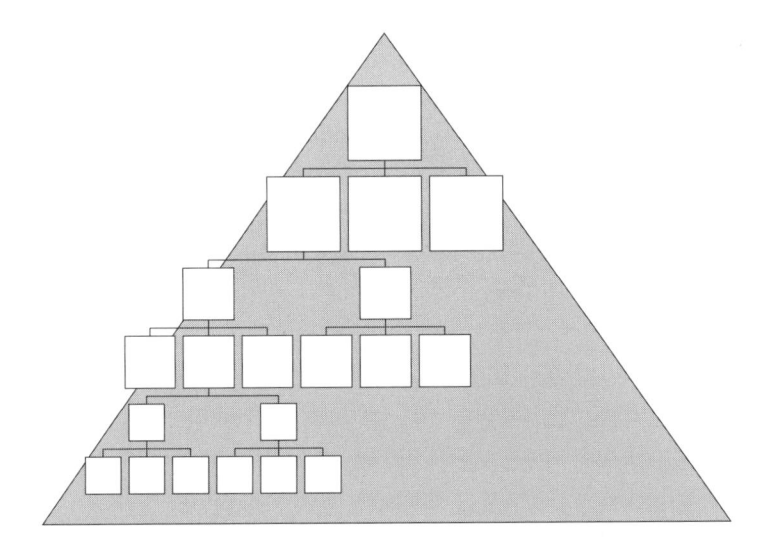

Emphasis on upward advancement also means that people have to give up doing what they're trained for (and love doing) in order to advance. Sales stars, designers, engineers, and others have to join the ranks of management to get promotions or pay increases. They may be damned good at one thing, and as a result be elevated into jobs where they're mediocre or worse. From being experts, they "progress" to being also-rans.

Territory becomes very important, and people become defensive about it. They treat connecting lines as if they were the only way to communicate. Crossing lines is strongly discouraged and can be politically dangerous.

The logic of yesterday's hierarchical structure was spot on. It might still make sense for some firms. But for many, these different times call for different answers. There are compelling reasons to turn things upside down:

1. Creating and keeping the right customers is management's most important task (because it's crucial to making a profit);
2. The purpose of any organization is to deliver value that (a) attracts customers, and (b) keeps them spending;
3. The job of the leader is to get results through people.

Organizational architecture has a major impact on organizational performance. But it's only partly about who sits where, who reports to whom, and what technology you use. *Far more important are soft factors such as leadership, communication, trust, ethics, integrity, transparency, accountability, and responsibility.* These, rather than structure, are what truly cause one company to beat another.

Everybody knows this. Every manager I talk to speaks in the same lofty terms about how they're priorities in his or her company. But don't believe it.

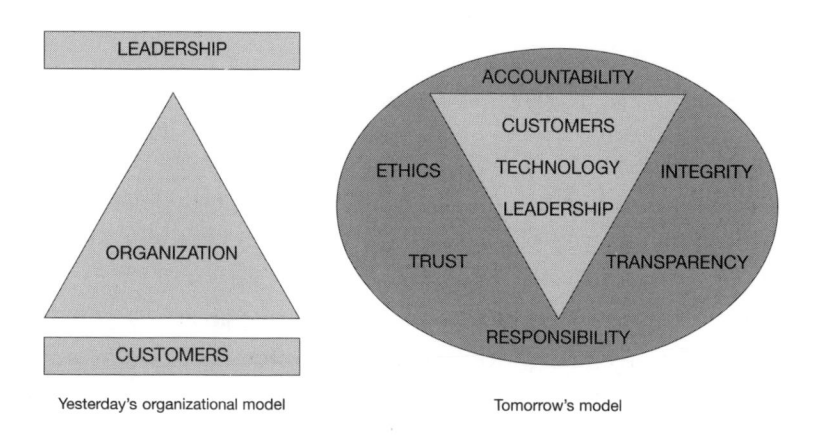

Yesterday's organizational model

Tomorrow's model

DESIGN FOR PERFORMANCE

Talking about your good intentions is not the same as *living* them. So before you talk about them yet again, just take a deep breath, think about what you're going to say ... and then shut up and *do* something.

Think about what it'll take to move from yesterday's organizational model to tomorrow's. Start thinking about your company as a results machine – and start thinking about what it really needs to look like in a rapidly changing, hyper-competitive world, where stakeholders are increasingly demanding and there's nowhere to hide.

Leadership

By one guesstimate, there are around 274 definitions of just what leadership is. But they all come down to one thing:

> *As a leader in any organization,*
> *your job is to get results through others.*
> *Make them shine,*
> *and they'll make you shine.*

Bringing out the best in just one person can make an astonishing impact. Bring out the best in a *team*, and the magic can't be measured. Create a community of champions, and there's no limit to what you – and they – can achieve.

In nature, systems organize themselves. In human affairs, someone has to do the organizing. And the more complex the world becomes, the more organizing there is to do.

Energetic forward movement is not natural for organizations. What is natural is *drift*. While some individuals might be quite enthusiastic about charging forward, groups tend to get so busy with their own dynamics that they slow down surprisingly fast. And they veer off course for almost any reason.

It's tempting to think that if you just get out of the way and let people "get on with it," they'll do the right things. Sometimes they will. Mostly, they won't. The idea of "self-managing teams" has merit, but it can only work when teams are focused, motivated, and – yes – *managed*.

Someone has to provide direction. Someone has to inspire action, assign tasks, align efforts, and encourage learning and the *sharing* of new knowledge. And someone has to ensure that new strengths get used to build new competitive advantages.

Often, there's only a fine line between making decisions yourself, and sharing or delegating them. Some decisions are yours to make. Sometimes, only the CEO, a senior executive, or a top team has the experience, knowledge, skill, or power to make a call. But a lot of decisions can and should be made by others. They're not only closer to the action, they're also more likely to implement their own decisions.

Empowerment is a wonderful idea and should be every leader's goal. But even the most empowered team needs a guiding hand. "The Boss" has always had a role, and still does, even in these idealistic, politically charged times.

Did you hire these idiots?

Look around your organization. How many of your people do you *really* value? How many do you think are idiots? Now ask yourself, where did the bozos come from? What makes the great performers that way? And why do so many people let you down?

If you're as quick as most managers to point fingers at the under-performers, stop and ask yourself:

- How did they get through the door?
- How were they selected from a pool of prospects?
- Who interviewed them?
- What process was followed?
- Why did you hire them? (Did they fool you or your colleagues who interviewed them?)
- What made you think they'd fit in and make the contribution you expected?
- Once they got in the door, what kind of induction did they get?
- What have you done to train and develop them?
- Do they understand your strategy?
- Are their roles clear?
- Do you manage them for success ... or failure?
- What incentives do you provide?

Some people will deliver what you expect – and more. Some will disappoint. You need to keep the first lot, and do whatever you can to help them do even better. The second lot need careful thought.

You might already know for sure that some of them are wrong for your company. Get rid of them fast. Don't torture yourself, and don't mislead them.

But there might be others you're not quite so sure about. Their performance isn't up to scratch – but you're not sure why. Proceed with extreme caution.

They might well be at fault. It might be a total waste of time trying to get different results from them. But maybe the problem lies elsewhere. Maybe they're in the wrong jobs. Maybe they lack the information they need. Maybe they're badly managed, demotivated, or inappropriately rewarded. If this is the case, you owe it to them and to your company to give them another chance and to do everything possible to fix things between you.

It's easy to write people off. It's a lot harder to turn them on. But the judgments you make about people can have serious implications for you and for them, and should be made with great care.

Conditions for greatness

There is no mystery about how to get the best out of people. When you've read everything available on the subject, and listened to every expert, you can sum up the formula in two words:

Purpose + Autonomy

If people are to produce results, they need to know what "results" means. In other words, where "the hill" is. Then, they need the freedom – and support – to invent the best possible way to the top.

I could say a lot more, but I'd be repeating myself. You could search for a better answer, but you won't find one. So ask yourself:
1. Is our purpose clear to all, and does everyone know what's expected of them, in *their* area of the business?
2. Have we done everything possible to unshackle people, stop wasting their time, and get out of their way?
3. Do we give them all they need to excel?

Purpose and autonomy give people a sense of self-worth and enable them to find meaning in their jobs. Nothing is more fulfilling. Nothing offers a better reason to get up in the morning and really want to be at work.

Meaning makes people volunteers. Put enough of those together, and you have a community of champions. And they'll make you … a leader!

Trust

Trust holds things together. It also oils the wheels of progress.

In a high-trust organization, you can focus on your work without having to watch your back. You don't have to ferret for information, and you can share it freely. Communication is open and honest. There are few hidden agendas. You can rely on people to do what they say.

In low-trust organizations, by contrast, you can never be sure that what you hear is true, or that you've got the whole story. Politics is rife. You have to decipher every utterance and action, and "get things in writing."

Organizations today rely increasingly on knowledge workers, and relationships are critically important. When trust is missing, things quickly come apart.

Unfortunately, trust is both fragile and fleeting. You can destroy it far more quickly and easily than you can create it. The risk that it will evaporate is one of the gravest threats any firm faces.

The only way to build trust is to act in a trustworthy way, consistently and over time. Individuals and organizations are judged by what they do, not what they say. It's essential that you live the philosophies you espouse and keep the promises you make.

The only way to build trust is to act in a trustworthy way, consistently and over time.

Corporate values statements scream, "Here's what we believe in." Yet all too often, no one takes them at their word. Insiders disregard them, and outsiders see them as puffery. And when there's the slightest lapse, they become a rod for managers' backs.

Trust is a very big deal indeed. Don't assume it will arrive on its own. Don't mess with it. Be wary of boasting about it in your mission statement, your annual report, or your advertising.

But do seize every opportunity to talk about it to your people. Keep emphasizing its importance. And take harsh action against anyone who violates it.

Building trust demands that you show others that you trust them without demanding that they trust you. This is obviously risky, but you have to give trust to get it.

In time, this most precious of assets will be central to "the way we do things around here." It'll be an unspoken element of your value proposition, a key factor in your competitiveness, and a reason for people to see your company as an employer of choice.

Teamwork

Magic people make a difference. But *teams* – now there's a topic for these interconnected times. Teamwork is big business.

It seems that everywhere you look, terrified people from Accounts are abseiling off cliffs; folks from Sales are doing the white water thing with their colleagues in Administration; and the R&D crowd are taking paintball potshots at the enemy from Distribution.

Some of this horsing around may put people in touch with their inner selves, some may teach them the value in collaborating with people they can't stand, and the impact of some of it may even carry over into the workplace. For a while. But mostly it's of questionable value. Its impact on the bottom line is minimal.

Teams fail to bond – or come apart – for many reasons. The people might be wrong. Or they might hate each other. Or they might never work out how to work together. But while these are the obvious areas to look for trouble, they're usually not the real cause of it.

The reason teams fail is that they have no reason to act like teams. They have no purpose. Their "hill" is not clear.

Flowing from this problem, they aren't sure what they should be doing. And they don't talk about it.

The antidote is simple. (And much cheaper than the teamwork gurus will let on.) There are three requirements:

Clear direction
+ Simple rules
+ Intense conversation

Are you disappointed? Don't be. If your company is like most others, there's hard work ahead. And a serious mind-shift.

People have to know what their team purpose is, or they'll do their own thing. You have to give them direction.

Simple rules frame what a team and its members must do. They provide the "tramlines" that keep activities on track. Two or three things are easier to communicate and remember than 30, and more likely to be adhered to. So best have just a few rules, and *be firm about them*, rather than try to enforce a long list that everyone will read to suit themselves, obey selectively, or ignore.

Intense conversation inspires creativity. When you put people close to each other and encourage them to talk, ideas bounce around and multiply. If they can *see* each other, sparks really fly. Bonding also occurs.

Teamwork is too important to leave to teams. Even more so if you're intent on creating "self-managing" teams. You have to provide leadership. And that means *direction* and *context*. Plus a healthy dose of pressure.

Reputation

With time, individuals, organizations, and countries develop reputations. Outsiders create mental impressions of them that are good, bad, or indifferent. A positive reputation can be worth a fortune; a negative one can cost a bundle.

It's remarkable, then, that managers are quite careless about building their firms' reputations. Sure, they spend a lot of money on advertising, and they might also have active public relations campaigns. Maybe they're into sponsorship, or corporate social responsibility programmes. But nothing hangs together. And to make things worse, there's a yawning gap between what's *said* and what's *done*.

Reputations are fragile things, rooted in trust. And, like trust, they take time to build but can be shattered in an instant. All around you, people are watching to see if you walk your talk. "Does this company deliver the profits it promised – and can we believe the numbers?" ... "Does its soap really wash whiter?" ... "Does it stand by its product warranties?" ... "Does it treat people as its 'most valuable resource'?" ... "Does it really care for the environment?" ....

Advertising has little credibility because customers have learned through bitter experience that companies exaggerate and lie about themselves. Slogans have no substance. PR messages are often seen as puffery. Even annual reports – where you'd think telling the truth would be quite important – are read with scepticism.

Reputation is an asset, and building a sound reputation is a matter of utmost importance. Yet while decisions about buying a new computer or building a factory are treated with great seriousness, decisions that impact directly on a company's reputation are taken far more lightly.

All too often, reputation-building is seen as merely a communications matter, when in fact it involves far more. And all too often, the task is left to powerless and inexperienced people – or the wrong ones. Senior communication executives don't get invited to key strategy meetings. Inexperienced brand managers brief young copywriters and art directors whose main aim is to win awards. Press releases are churned out by hacks who charge by the word.

> All too often, reputation-building is seen as merely a communications matter, when in fact it involves far more.

So what to do instead? Some suggestions:

1. Get your strategic conversation right. Your company's reputation is, after all, an extension of it. What you talk about inside your walls translates into action ... and that's what gets seen outside.
2. Be clear about the impression you wish to convey, both inside and outside your organization. Be specific about the image you want to build. Make sure all your people know what you want the world to think. Equip them to deliver on your promises.
3. Test all communications against the themes of your strategic conversation. Be sure that they reinforce each other and amplify your message, and don't water it down or blur it.
4. Check that what you're saying is heard the way you mean it to be, and that the effect is what you expect. Don't assume you're either

getting through to your various audiences or making the right impression. Ask them for feedback.
5. Stay "on message." When your communication efforts are all over the show, those on the receiving end will get a blurry picture. Global marketers like to talk about "one sight, one sound, one sell." It's good advice.
6. Act with integrity. What you *say*, stakeholders will experience as just hot air; what they *actually* experience leaves an indelible impression. No amount of camouflage can hide the reality of what you *are*.

Integrity

Corporate shenanigans have made integrity a crucial factor in every area of life. But the word has been so bandied about that it's been devalued.

What does it mean? What must you do to be seen to "act with integrity?"

The dictionary tells us that integrity is a synonym for honesty and that both rest on truthfulness, but that integrity has the added dimension of "uprightness." And who would argue that organizations in both the private and public sectors could do with a lot more of these traits?

But there's another way to think about integrity. As Shakespeare put it, "To thine own self be true." Be yourself. Dig deep into yourself, and think about who you are and what you stand for. Then, act out that view, in everything you do.

Or put it like this:

*To have integrity is to accept who you are,
to honour your uniqueness,
to live your own life in your own way,
and not to pretend you are someone else
in order to win approval.*

When there's a straight line from what you believe to how you act, people don't have to waste time and frustrate themselves in trying to "decode" you. When "what you see is what you get," you don't have to waste your time ducking and diving and trying to be what you're not.

Integrity is important in people. It's important, too, in companies and their offerings. The products and services you sell – and the way you brand them – should reflect your company's deepest values.

If you fail in this, there will be a costly disconnect between what you are and what you promise. Customers will find you out. And they'll spread the dirt.

If, however, you succeed in walking your talk, you'll be likely to earn respect, grow your reputation, and win customers and profits.

Culture

When things go wrong in a firm, the cry goes up, "The problem is our culture. We must change it." This sounds logical, so consultants are called in and comprehensive change processes are put on the table. In no time, there's a cottage industry of personality and aptitude assessments, one-on-one counselling, workshops, and training programmes.

People are hired, fired, and moved around. Naturally, a new vision and mission are drafted. The performance management system has to be replaced. A new incentive plan is put in place.

And the result is ... disappointment.

If you talk to people who sell culture change, they'll assure you it's easy. "Want to pull it off by the end of the year? ... No problem." "Want to make everyone customer-obsessed? ... Sure." "Want innovation from everyone? ... Just name the date."

Don't believe it. Changing culture is actually extremely hard and can take a hell of a long time.

Changing our own minds is a challenge we all wrestle with. Changing lots of others is another problem entirely. In both cases, world views are the problem.

Changing culture is actually extremely hard and can take a hell of a long time.

Culture is the sum of an organization's assumptions, beliefs, values, and actions.

When people work together, they brainstorm ideas, make things, deal with customers, hassle with the bank, fight with each other, and so on. As this happens, their collective tape rolls and records everything. Gradually, a formula for the group's survival – and hopefully for success – gets laid down.

Much of what they learn becomes a taken-for-granted *world view*, which in turn forms the bedrock for all decisions and actions.

The further they travel into the future, the harder it gets to unpack that formula. Just when did the vision become something they all implicitly accepted? How did the values, honed so painfully in workshops and printed on laminated pocket cards, become real gut-level beliefs? What caused earnest debate about "the way we do things around here" to become the way things actually get done?

See the problem? See what you're up against when you want to change culture? Organizational memory doesn't get wiped out and replaced overnight. It's very sticky.

So what to do?

Begin by thinking of culture in terms of cause and effect. The effect you want is a change in behaviour. But what will cause it?

The answer is well known. Psychologists have told us for a hundred years or so that personal change begins with a change in what you *do*, not what you *think*. Change your actions, and your heart and mind follow. Try to change your mind first … and you'll be at it forever.

*Culture causes people to behave in a certain way.
At the same time, their behaviour
shapes the culture.
So culture is both a cause and a consequence.*

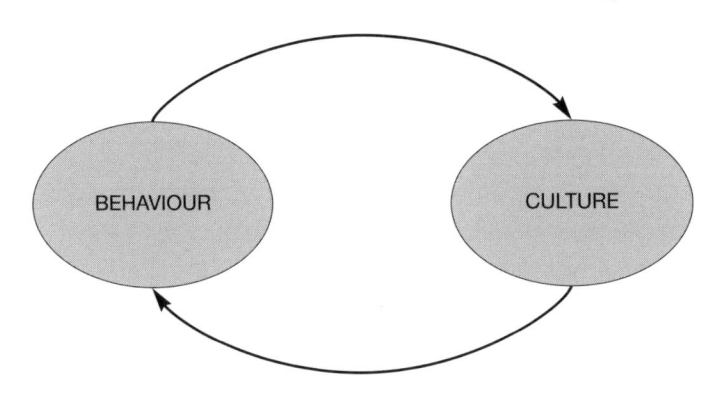

```
   BEHAVIOUR  ⟶  CULTURE
              ⟵
```

The lesson: if you think you need to change your company's culture, tackle the project from the right direction. Focus on changing *work*. Get your people to do different things ... and do things differently. Change their priorities. Set tight new deadlines. Push for rapid results. Demand regular progress reports.

In the short term, you'll inspire new performance. With time, attitudes, assumptions, values, and habits will change. And one day you'll be able to report that while all of you were working, a new culture was born. You have new tapes in your heads.

*Culture does exist in organizations.
It matters hugely.
Over time, it can cause a firm to fly ... or to fail.
But culture is one of the least manageable
factors in any organization.
Changing it fast is virtually impossible.*

Climate

Organizational culture gets a huge amount of attention. By contrast, organizational climate is a poor cousin and largely ignored. This is strange, given that changing culture is tougher than you think, while changing climate is quite easy and the impact of climate on performance is enormous.

Climate is the "weather system" that determines how people feel at work. It is determined by two things:
1. **Hygiene** factors – working conditions, pay, benefits, etc.;
2. **Context** factors – direction, support, trust, respect, communication, and so on.

Hygiene factors obviously matter. They're "the basics," and you have to get them right or they'll be constant irritants to everyone.

Context factors drive performance. When people feel that they get these things in the workplace, they're likely to act positively. When these factors are absent or weak, underperformance and dysfunctional behaviour are to be expected.

How would you describe your organization's climate today?

How would you like to describe it?

DIRECTION		PERFORMANCE
SUPPORT		ALIGNMENT
TRUST		COOPERATION
RESPECT		"VOLUNTEERISM"
COMMUNICATION		RESPECT
OPENNESS		ENERGY
INTEGRITY		TRUST
STRETCH		INTEGRITY
		STRETCH

Fix the basics. Change the context. Commit yourself to some new behaviours now ... and watch how fast other people change, too.

Pivotal people

At times, the challenge of change can seem overwhelming. Where to start? All those people to get on board! What first? *Who* first?

Well, start by recognizing that you don't have to change everyone on day one. In fact, doing so is impossible. What you do need is for a critical mass of them to buy in to your new direction soon. And the best way to get that is to focus on the "pivotal people."

Every organization has them. They're the movers and shakers – the ones who influence the rest.

Some get their power from their positions: they're senior managers, for example, or departmental heads. Others have special skills or knowledge. Another lot are great networkers, with valuable relationships both inside and outside the organization. And always there will be some "political animals" – those with Machiavellian instincts who are forever sniffing the wind, scavenging for rumours, and tossing hints like grenades. They're "economical with the truth," they cunningly mould half-formed thoughts into full-blown forecasts, and they distort facts to suit their ends.

The point is, love 'em or hate 'em, these individuals have the sway you need to get things moving. By leveraging their strengths, you make the 80/20 principle work for you. Get them on your side early, and they'll bring others with them. Ignore them, or – God forbid – overlook them, and you can expect trouble.

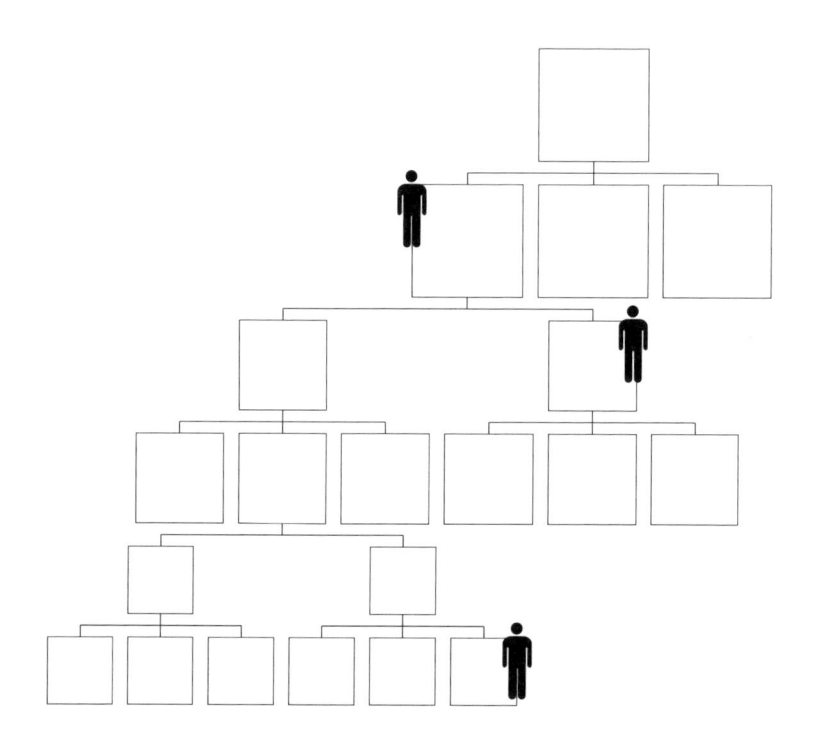

Diversity

Around the world, workforces are becoming more diverse. People of various colours and races are filling jobs at all levels. There are more women at work. A massive social revolution is under way.

And about time, too, many people would say. The *moral* case for diversity is indisputable. There is also a *social* case (everyone should have the same job opportunities), a *legal* case (laws are in place to enforce change), and a *business* case (customers, workers, and society are all multi-hued). The question is no longer, "Should we do something about diversity?" but rather, "*What* must we do, and *how*?"

Those in favour of changes in business say that diversity adds real value by providing different perspectives, richer ideas, and better knowledge of customers.

Their argument sounds logical. Those benefits are worth pursuing. But don't think they'll come without special effort.

Diversity is no longer a choice. But simply tossing a disparate bunch of people together won't give you the benefits you expect. Hoping for the best is no way to get it. Making diversity work – as with anything else – requires serious changes in the way you do things.

When people from different backgrounds engage with each other, they bring lots of baggage with them. They may be reluctant to speak out. When they do, they may be confrontational, abrasive, and unconstructive. Or they might strive so hard to fit in that they add nothing.

Their insights might be misunderstood, unappreciated, or ignored. Their creativity can easily be stifled. Grandstanding is common, and charges of "racism" are an easy defence against criticism.

Working as a team is never easy. Even homogenous groups have problems. Mixed groups are worse.

Two things will help you make diversity work:
1. A set of guiding principles or rules;
2. An effective strategic conversation.

The guiding principles provide a frame for behaviour. They make it clear to all what is acceptable and what's not. The best way to get to them is to get everyone involved. This lessens the chances of anyone who steps out of line saying, "I don't agree with your rules."

> **The question is no longer, "Should we do something about diversity?" but rather, "*What* must we do, and *how*?"**

These are ones that usually come up:
1. Respect each other;
2. Accept others' views;
3. Be open and honest;
4. Everyone participate;
5. Be positive and constructive;
6. Focus on issues, not personalities.

If you think these are obvious, you're right. Most people want pretty much the same things when they interact with each other.

The same behaviours are necessary for a fruitful strategic conversation. By laying down the ground rules for *how* you'll talk to each other, you can get on with the nitty-gritty issues of *what* to talk about.

Strategic conversation homes in on the key themes that will make your company successful. It tells people, "This is what we must focus on." And because it helps them understand the priorities, and understand their roles, it lets them contribute constructively to the team and perform better themselves.

Strategic conversation is not just a tool for getting to a clear strategy and communicating it clearly. It is also a tool for managing diversity.

Creative thinking

How many ideas did you have today that will actually affect how much money you make? How much time did you spend *thinking*?

If you don't set out deliberately to find new things to do, and new and better ways to do them, don't be surprised if you seldom make breakthroughs. Thinking is work. So work at it.

How many ideas came from your people? How good were those ideas? Why weren't there more? Why weren't there more of a better *quality*? How do you encourage people to think constantly about what your company can do differently and better – and what else you could do?

Some ideas sneak up while you're not looking. They arrive out of nowhere. If you're lucky, you can write them down and act on them before they vanish again. So keep pen and paper handy, and make a habit of thinking about your thoughts. It's no good waiting for inspiration if you're not alert and ready to capture and manage what comes.

The busier you get, the less time you're likely to spend on creative thinking. It pays to constantly check that you're doing what matters most. Be disciplined about your chores; but be equally disciplined about making and managing ideas.

There are many recipes for generating ideas. But remarkably, there have been few new ideas about how to do it since John Dewey wrote his classic book *How We Think* in 1910. Most formulas come down to these suggestions:

1. Define your problem precisely;
2. Turn it upside down;
3. Reverse it;
4. Look at it from someone else's perspective;
5. Make it bigger;
6. Make it smaller;
7. Change its colour;
8. Combine things;
9. Borrow from something else;
10. Add something;
11. Subtract something;
12. Set a deadline;
13. Persevere.

If you think about it, creativity is simply about connecting things in new ways. Sometimes it happens by accident. But in business, you need to be more deliberate. You can't hang around hoping for that "Aha!" moment when suddenly you see things differently. You have to produce new ideas on command.

Creativity is simply about connecting things in new ways.

The key is to have plenty of bits and pieces of information and experience in your head to call up when you need them. After all, without lots of "loose stuff" in your head, you've got nothing to connect!

David Ogilvy, the legendary adman, used to say that he always looked for people "with a well furnished mind." That's a lovely way to describe what every company needs.

Your business environment can be designed to encourage creative thinking. Architectural features and furniture play an important role. Colours, pictures, personal items, quotes on walls, and so on can all enliven a workspace and provoke conversation.

But far more important is the *mental* space you create for people. It's a product of the priorities you set and of where you put your resources. Also, of the things you say and the questions you ask – in other words, of your strategic conversation.

Some thought starters:
- "Is there another way?"
- "What else …?"
- "Who else …?"
- "What if …?"
- "What more …?"
- "Why do we …?"
- "Why don't we …?"

Everyone a genius

How many really smart people do you employ? Have you any idea?

Most managers haven't a clue about their people's brainpower. They have no idea who knows what, who their "out-of-the-box" thinkers are, or where breakthrough ideas are likely to come from. In fact, too often they lump most people together as dimwits.

Result: they don't expect much, they don't challenge people enough, and they try to do all the creative thinking themselves. Which, if you think about it, is pretty damned stupid.

No one has an exclusive hold on good ideas. Everyone is potentially a revolutionary. Surprising insights can come from anywhere.

The best way to get ideas from people is to ask them daily: "What did you do differently and better today?" "What will you do differently and better tomorrow?" "How can I help you?" The personal touch works far better than any system or structured process.

Suggestion schemes fail because people quickly discover no one cares about their suggestions. Too often, they volunteer ideas that they think are important, but which get ignored.

Reflection on learning

Business schools typically use case studies to try to simulate the complex thinking processes that occur in companies. When students present and debate their views, the professor teases out their arguments to (a) test their logic, and (b) show that various "solutions" are possible. It's a rich learning experience, but not complete. To get maximum value from the process, students need to spend time afterwards *reflecting* on what happened and how, and what it meant.

The workplace, of course, is a live case study – the real thing. Reflection about what happens there is even more important than it is in the classroom.

You can accelerate the development of both your own and other people's skills by creating an environment in which it's normal and safe to sit back and ask, "What's happening here?" ... "Why are we talking this way?" ... "What assumptions are influencing us?" ... "How are we doing in dealing with this issue?"

Post-mortems, too, can be catalysts for growth. But the intention must be clear: it is to *learn*, not lament.

On the one hand, you need to learn about the effect of a particular choice – "We did this, so this happened." At a deeper level, the issue is *how and why you got to that decision* – "We talked about it like this ... we considered these factors, but not those ... this person won support for these reasons ... this one backed down, and here's why" ... and so on.

Open and honest – and deliberate – reflection like this makes all experience a learning event. It can also help pull a team together, as people realize that they have lots to gain from each other, and that robust conversation is both great fun and good for you.

The limits of freedom

Over the past 20 years or so, the notion of freedom has taken firm hold in management-speak. If you weren't paying attention, you'd think it really had become an important value in organizational life.

Executives are told to "let go" ... "empower people" ... "set them free" ... "liberate them from bureaucracy." They make stirring speeches that exhort folks to "break all rules," "push the envelope," and so on. And their company conferences have themes like "Everything's possible" or "No limits."

This is all good, stirring stuff. But mostly it's just hot air. And often, it's bad advice.

Empowerment is a buzzword beloved by the politically correct crowd. In theory, it's exactly the right thing to aim for. In practice, though, it works only in limited circumstances.

Empowerment means you equip an individual to do whatever she's hired for, then let her loose to do it her own way. Seven things make it hard to do:

1. People must have the basic abilities their job demands;
2. They must be trained and retrained;
3. Their goals must be clear;
4. They must be given space to invent their own way into the future;
5. They must get whatever information, resources, and support they need;
6. They must get fast feedback on their performance;
7. They must align their efforts with those of others.

How would you rate your organization on these seven factors? If it's like most others, your score will be dismal. So forget the rhetoric. Fix the basics. Put the building blocks in place that will let you walk the talk sometime in the future.

For people to do their best, they need to know:
1. What to do (the task);
2. Why to do it (its purpose);
3. How to do it (the method);
4. How well to do it (standards).

They also need feedback to know:
5. How well they're doing.

How do your people rate against these questions? How do you rate in providing answers?

Empowerment depends on communication. And once is not enough. You have to communicate and communicate ... and communicate again. Over and over until you want to scream.

The goal is to be able to let go. The reality is that you have to stick around, and keep talking.

You don't have to have the best ideas first. But try to implement them best – and fastest. Then keep improving them ahead of the pack.

Start slow, finish fast

There's no question: the clockspeed of business is accelerating. Things are happening faster and faster. Speed is a critical competitive weapon.

But don't get carried away.

Too fast can be just as dangerous as too slow. Get too excited about a new project, and you risk barging ahead with too little preparation. Keep moving, and you might not learn as much as you should, or be able to turn your new insights into sensible action.

Too fast can be just as dangerous as too slow.

Just as teenagers take time to "chill" between school, dates, and kinetic nights in the disco, so do we all need to balance our lives. Quiet time lets you gather strength for the next burst of activity. Relaxing with a book or at a movie lets you rebuild your body and refresh your mind.

Athletes don't try to reach peak performance on day one. They practise themselves to perfection. They pace themselves carefully, until mentally they're "in the zone" and physically they can push right through pain.

Prepare your company well for challenges. Make sure that "the basics" are sound before you go for the big leap. Warm people up for what's ahead. Then, when you move, move fast.

The best time for decisions

Running a business is like living in a pressure cooker. Companies are in a race to the future. Everyone wants things done "now!" Deadlines drive a sense of urgency. Decisiveness is a highly admired trait.

And so it should be.

But wait. There is a best time for everything. And "this minute" might not be it.

Any time you face a decision, you have certain information to hand. Right now, all you really know is what's past. The future is just a bunch of assumptions.

One minute from now, you'll know more than you do at the moment. In a week, a month, or ten years' time, you'll again be in a different place – and you'll also have different information to work with.

Some decisions *do* have to be made instantly. When you face one of those, don't delay. Inform yourself as well as possible, think through the issues as well as you can, consider all your options, and then act.

> One minute from now, you'll know more than you do at the moment.

But when you have more time – and that's *most* of the time – take advantage of it:

- Do your homework;
- Call for new information;
- Open your mind to fresh insights;
- Bounce your thoughts off other people;
- If you can, try small, low-cost experiments to test your thinking.

Being decisive is vital in a "fast clockspeed" world. But make it a golden rule to never lay a bet until there's a reason to do it. Never make up your mind about anything today if you can sensibly put off doing so until tomorrow.

Slow decisions are often the smartest ones.
Doing nothing can often be best.

Follow through

The right things generally do not happen by themselves. With few exceptions, even the best people will let you down when it comes to execution. No matter how clear you are about setting goals, no matter how much you trust your team to deliver on them, and no matter how much you believe in standing back and letting them get on with the job, goals will be missed, deadlines will drift by, and the same actions will appear again and again on your "to do" list.

Effective execution is a skill that combines art with discipline.

You need to motivate people to meet their commitments – and even more so if you want them to go the extra mile. This tests your powers of persuasion, your coaching ability, and your passion.

You also need to be firm in stating your expectations, uncompromising about standards, and tough when the wheels spin. Right from the start, you have to make it clear that the goals people agree to are etched in stone; anything less will not do. And you need to follow through to check that things are progressing as they should.

In some cases, you can allow people space. It's enough to touch base with them at fairly long intervals, to show that you're interested in what's happening and are keeping tabs on it. In other cases, you have to literally get into micro-management mode, checking, questioning, and pushing hard so there's no doubt about your seriousness – or the consequences of failure.

Be firm in stating your expectations, uncompromising about standards, and tough when the wheels spin.

The 30-day planning process is a systematic way of ensuring execution. It may seem like hard work, but it keeps the heat on and keeps everyone informed. The plans they put forward should be treated as contracts. But it sometimes pays to add extra pressure by writing brief notes to key people after these reviews, reminding them of what they agreed to. Then, when you see them again, you can pull out your notes and use them to show that bullshit is not a good idea.

To push the boundaries of corporate performance, you have to unleash the imagination and spirit of people.
Extraordinary changes and improvements are possible when you tap into the human potential within your walls.

Your point of view

One thing today's leaders would do well to remember is that *most people want strong leadership.* They want someone to make the big decisions. They want direction, guidance, and support. Anything less scares the hell out of them. They don't follow wimps.

Leaders need a point of view – about the world, about what's right for their company, about what behaviours are acceptable and what's not. They need to be sure of their "hill," and confident about how to get there.

"Because I say so" is not a point of view. It's brainless and disrespectful bullying, and is unlikely to get you anywhere.

A point of view needs to project thoughtfulness and certainty. It needs to provide direction and inspire confidence. Developing one is never easy. But the effort you put into doing it will pay off hugely.

> A point of view needs to project thoughtfulness and certainty.

If you already have a point of view about your business, express it. Let people know how you arrived at your strategy, why you believe in it, what you expect from them. And make clear what you stand for and what you believe in, what you'll tolerate and what you won't.

If you *don't* have a point of view – or if you're not sure what it is – best you spend time thinking about this crucial matter soon, and start clarifying your position in your own mind and in the minds of the people who rely on you.

You need true believers to conquer your "hill." Give them something to believe in.

Draw a line in the sand

Perhaps the most valuable tool you have is this one:

Recognize it? It's a line in the sand. It says, "So far, and no further."

Try drawing a few of them today. With people who whine or push their pet projects too hard. With customers who demand too much. With suppliers who let you down. With bullying bank managers, pesky social activists, and nosy media.

Make up your own mind about what's good for your business. Explain your intentions clearly, simply, and firmly. Stand up for yourself. Be assertive.

Some give and take is always necessary in life. But when you do all the giving and someone else does all the taking, it's time to call a halt.

You will be tested.
So when you draw that line in the sand,
be sure you really mean it.

*Don't move it, erase it,
or draw another one under pressure.*

The move after next

The next move you make becomes a stepping stone to the future. It commits you to some degree, so it warrants careful thought.

What do you want to do the step after next? And the one after that?

Look ahead. Imagine you are where you want to be in six months, or five years. Look backwards. Now, does your next step make sense?

The strategy staircase

If you've read this far, you probably have a lot to do. But face it: you can't do it all at once or right away. You can't afford to and you don't have the resources. (Remember the "ten-buck test"!) You have to take one step at a time, putting one thing in place and then another. You have to pace yourself.

Think about it as building a staircase. Lay down one brick ... and then another ... and another. Make sure each one is firmly in place. And that each layer offers the right support to the one on top of it.

By breaking your strategy down this way, you reduce it to chunks of work you can get your hands around. It becomes doable. You make important progress possible. You give your team plenty of reasons to celebrate success. And before you know it, you're where you want to go.

YEAR 3

YEAR 2

YEAR 1

THE STRATEGY STAIRCASE

Appendix 1

The "5Ss" framework is based on the reality that the future changes constantly and fast, organizations operate in a world of many stakeholders with different agendas, and value is increasingly created through knowledge and relationships.

This revolutionary management tool gives you an insightful view of what you must do to succeed against increasingly hostile competition. It helps you think about issues that the traditional value chain ignores. And it takes account of the fact that while many activities are important to success, they're not worth much until you "pull them all together."

Use these questions to analyse your current business, and to hunt for opportunities:

1. SENSING

How do we know what's happening in our world – both outside and inside our organization – and how do we exploit what we learn?

1.1. Do we get enough *right* information about:
- Key political, economic, social, and technological trends?
- Customers and markets?
- Competitors (and possible substitutes)?
- Suppliers?
- New business trends (management ideas, organizational design, information technology, production, logistics, customer service, etc.)?
- Factors *within* our organization that affect performance (management style, climate, skills development, performance management, etc.)?
- Innovations (R&D projects, processes, product and service developments, etc.)?

1.2. What sources do we use for information?
1.3. How reliable are they?
1.4. What others are available?

2. SOURCING

What inputs do we need, where and how do we get them, and is there a better way?

2.1. Finance?
2.2. People?
2.3. Equipment?
2.4. Facilities?
2.5. Components?
2.6. Sub-assemblies?
2.7. Information?
2.8. Services?
2.9. Support?

3. SERVING

What value do we deliver, and how?

3.1. Is our target audience clear?
3.2. Do we understand their wants, needs, and behaviours?
3.3. How are they likely to change? (What will they buy tomorrow?)
3.4. Is our value proposition clear and relevant?
3.5. How do we deliver what we promise? (Production processes, logistics, marketing, administration, service, support, recycling/disposal, etc.)
3.6. Is our whole team focused on this goal?
3.7. Do they have the information, resources, and support they need?
3.8. How else could we push the "value envelope"?
3.9. How defensible is our situation?
3.10. What substitutes are likely? (When? Where from? Impact?)

4. SYMBIOSIS

Who must we influence, and how do we win their "votes"?

4.1. Have we clearly identified the stakeholders who matter to us?
4.2. Do we understand their needs, motives, intentions, and strategies?
4.3. What else must we learn about them?

4.4. Are we clear about what we expect from each of them?
4.5. Have we made our strategy clear to them?
4.6. How do we communicate with them?
4.7. How likely are they to support us – and why?
4.8. Who else should we communicate with to influence them?
4.9. What threatens our relationships?

5. SYNTHESIS

How do we pull things together so we can execute our plans impeccably?

5.1. Do we make things simple, so people can understand them?
5.2. Do we "unbundle" ideas, activities, and goals into "bite-sized chunks," so they can be effectively explained and properly understood?
5.3. Are our priorities, goals, and action plans known and understood by everyone who impacts our performance?
5.4. Is our "strategic conversation" simple and clear?
5.5. Do we work hard to break down boundaries to conversation and barriers to collaboration?
5.6. Do we follow through to check progress and get useful feedback?
5.7. Do we deliberately and consistently share what we learn?

Appendix 2

Use the 7Ps questionnaire to design a business model that will make your firm a true "results machine."

1. PURPOSE

Why do we exist?

1.1. Whom do we serve? (Consider all stakeholders.)
- How do we rank them by influence/importance?

1.2. What value do we deliver to our stakeholders?
- Product/service benefits?
- Technology/processes?
- Image?
- Relationship? (Knowledge, distribution, association, etc.)
- Financial? (Costs, profits.)

1.3. Why do we matter to them?
- Why would they be worse off without us?
- Why should they want us to survive and grow?

1.4. What is our ambition?
- Growth in sales, market share, profits, etc.?
- Innovation?
- People?
- Contribution to society?
- Environmental impact?

2. PHILOSOPHIES

What beliefs guide us? (Consider the following issues.)

2.1. Strategy–
- 2.1.1. The process (concepts, models, theories) we use?
- 2.1.2. Our business model?
- 2.1.3. Who we involve in creating strategy?
- 2.1.4. Sharing information?
- 2.1.5. How we define "success"?

- 2.1.6. How we decide what's best?
- 2.1.7. Our performance measures?
- 2.1.8. How we make trade-offs or sacrifices?
- 2.1.9. The way we implement our strategy?

2.2. People–
- 2.2.1. The kinds of people we seek?
  - Skills/attitudes?
  - Diversity?
  - Age?
- 2.2.2. Their induction into our organization?
- 2.2.3. The training and development we provide?
- 2.2.4. Performance management?
- 2.2.5. Our reward programmes?
- 2.2.6. Our management style?
- 2.2.7. Communication?
- 2.2.8. Our expectations of them?
- 2.2.9. Their involvement in outside activities?
- 2.2.10. Facilities we provide for them?
- 2.2.11. Our responsibility for their welfare?
- 2.2.12. Our responsibility towards their families?

2.3. Processes–
- 2.3.1. High tech vs. high touch?
- 2.3.2. Levels of technology investment?
- 2.3.3. Safety?
- 2.3.4. Quality?
- 2.3.5. Productivity?
- 2.3.6. Environmental preservation?
- 2.3.7. Constant improvement?
- 2.3.8. Outsourcing?

2.4. Competitors–
- 2.4.1. How carefully we watch them?
- 2.4.2. What we allow them to do?
- 2.4.3. Copying or leapfrogging them?

- 2.4.4. How aggressively we respond?
- 2.4.5. How fast we respond?
- 2.4.6. The lengths we'll go to in order to beat them?

2.5. Social responsibility–
- 2.5.1. Investing in education, welfare, housing, art, etc.?
- 2.5.2. Involvement in external activities?
- 2.5.3. Environmental issues?
- 2.5.4. Consumerism?

3. PRODUCTS

What do we offer, what is our difference, and why does it matter?

- 3.1. What need does it fill, or what problem does it solve?
- 3.2. What makes it different?
- 3.3. Why does that difference matter?
- 3.4. For how long will this difference matter?
- 3.5. How far have we pushed the "value envelope"?
- 3.6. What improvements/changes are needed (and when)?
- 3.7. How defensible is our situation?
- 3.8. What substitutes are likely? (When? Where from? Impact?)
- 3.9. Which way are sales headed?

4. POSITIONING

Who is our customer and how do we want to be perceived?

- 4.1. Who is our "right" customer?
- 4.2. What do customers know and feel about our company/product?
- 4.3 How do they see us relative to our competitors?
- 4.4. What would we like them to think?
- 4.5. What can we do to change their perceptions?
- 4.6. Do we promote brands or sell products?
- 4.7. What stops competitors from making the same claims?
- 4.8. What must we do to defend our positioning?

5. PROCESSES
What do we do – and how do we do it?

5.1. Why do we do the things we do?
5.2. Does everything we do add value/cut costs?
5.3. Do we know where value is destroyed and costs are added?
5.4. Is there a better way?
5.5. Are we urgently and aggressively seeking that better way?
5.6. What should we give up?

6. PEOPLE
Who do we employ and how do we manage them?

6.1. Do we have "magic people" in all pivotal jobs?
6.2. Do our hiring practices enhance our competitiveness?
6.3. Is our induction adequate?
6.4. Do our training and development programmes equip people with appropriate new skills and attitudes?
6.5. Do we make people *feel* important ... or do we *make them* important by giving them information, resources, and responsibility?
6.6. Do we expose them to new ideas – and listen to their ideas?
6.7. Do we stretch them by giving them important assignments?
6.8. Do they think we see them as an asset or a cost?
6.9. Do they feel they can speak their minds – and do they speak up?
6.10. Is the corporate conversation "nourishing" or "toxic"?
6.11. What incentives do we offer – and are they adequate?
6.12. Are career paths clear and meaningful?

7. PARTNERS
Who will help us reach our goals and how do we manage these relationships?

7.1. Have we identified possible partners, defined how they could aid us, and made contact with them?
7.2. Do they understand our strategy?

7.3. Do they know what we expect of them?
7.4. Do we agree on how we'll work together?
7.5. What is the level of trust between us?
7.6. How much information do we share with them?
7.7. How good are our personal relationships?
7.8. Are the rewards balanced?
7.9. Who is driving improvement (us or them)?